THE PRESENT AGE

SØREN KIERKEGAARD

THE PRESENT AGE
AND
OF THE DIFFERENCE
BETWEEN A GENIUS AND
AN APOSTLE

Translated and with an Introduction by
ALEXANDER DRU

COLLINS

THE FONTANA LIBRARY
THEOLOGY AND PHILOSOPHY

First published by the Oxford University Press,
First issued in the Fontana Library, 1962

CONTENTS

CONTENTS

INTRODUCTION
BY
ALEXANDER DRU

There is no work, Léon Brunschwicg writes in his preface to the *Pensées*, which is more in need of a commentary, and there is no writer so impatient of the commentator's intervention, as Pascal. His words apply equally to Kierkegaard: but in Kierkegaard's case the dilemma is not unresolvable. He took infinite pains to correct and forestall misunderstanding; he wrote profusely about his own work, and he can be allowed, in a large measure, to be his own commentator: to provide the light in which the purpose of his work as a whole should be seen, and the criterion by which it should be interpreted. He has, in fact, supplied the objective point of view from which to approach his daunting and subjective work. It is given briefly and clearly in the two essays which follow, where he analyses the historical perspective in which his work should be read and the situation in and for which he wrote. And if there were any doubt as to the propriety of reading them in this way, there is his own statement to the effect that his importance as a writer would ultimately depend upon the accuracy with which he diagnosed the exigencies of the present age:

'The individual' is the category through
which, from a religious point of view, our
age, our race, and its history must pass . . .
My possible importance is undoubtedly
linked to that category. My writings may of
course, be forgotten, like those of many
another writer. But if that was the right
category, and if everything was in order with
that category . . . in that case I shall endure
and my writings with me.

Conversely, it can now be said that, if
Kierkegaard leapt into fame after being
ignored for more than a century after his birth
it was because his diagnosis was correct in
essentials. What better introduction to his
work than the pages in which he summarised
his view of the present age?

The Present Age, as given here, is the second
half of a review of a novel by a writer well-
known in her day, whose identity was not,
however, disclosed until after her death. Fru
Gyllemburg was the mother of J. L. Heiberg,
the most distinguished litterateur of his generation in Copenhagen, who had at one time
encouraged Kierkegaard and published his first
political articles. Her novel, *The Two Ages*,
provided Kierkegaard with a peg on which to
hang his ideas. *Of the Difference between a Genius
and an Apostle* was written at about the same
time, between 1846 and 1847. It formed part
of a voluminous study of the case of the

Reverend Adolph Peter Adler, but was sub-
sequently re-written and published separately.[1]
Adler had at one time been a follower of Hegel,
until called by private ' revelations ' to spread
the Gospel. Kierkegaard was fascinated by
Adler and the difficulties which he caused to
the Established Religion. He saw in him not
only an example of misguided enthusiasm
further confused by a complete misunderstanding of the present age, but a caricature
of his own position. Between them, the two
essays provide a general view of the historical
background in which ' the category of the
individual ' emerged and against which its
significance becomes clear. They were not to be
regarded as part of his *oeuvre*, but were written
as though from outside it and intended as
introductory.

The ' present age ' is the phase of history
inaugurated by the Revolution considered not
only as a political event but as a change
affecting every sphere of life and thought: a
metamorphosis accomplished in man's self-
consciousness by virtue of which he attained
his majority. Most striking in its immediate
effect in the political sphere, it was no less
important in the cultural sphere of manners,
morals, art and philosophy. Indeed it was not

[1] The ' book on Adler ' was translated by Walter Lowrie:
On Authority and Revelation. Princeton University Press, 1955.

primarily an external revolution in the ordering
of life, but an inner revolution in how men
viewed politics, religion and culture in relation
to one another. In this cultural sense it was the
end of Christendom, and it was in order
to obtain recognition of that fact that
Kierkegaard wrote the bitter pamphlets
published during the last months of his life:
Attack on Christendom—and not as is sometimes
said, ' attack on Christianity '. The mediaeval
synthesis—the global cultural tradition we call
Christendom—no longer existed; not because
men were less Christian, or because there were
fewer Christians, but because the synthesis,
that particular accord between religion, politics
and culture, had outlived its day. The present
age is neither an indifferent copy, a decadent
form, nor a disorderly version of what went
before. Nor could it be regarded without gross
over-simplification merely as better or worse
than what had preceded. It was radically new.
And the first business of those who wished to
defend Christianity, no less than of those
who wished to bury it, was to acknowledge
the fact, and not to allow themselves to be
hoodwinked into talking in irrelevant terms
and about a situation which no longer
existed.

Historically, the cultural revolution is called
the Enlightenment, the final phase in the
secularisation of the European tradition which

began with the Renaissance and gradually broke up the mediaeval synthesis. The political revolution had declared the Rights of Man; the cultural revolution the emancipation of thought and, at first sight, in the religious sphere, the bankruptcy of Christianity. One stream of the Enlightenment, notably in France, had stressed the anti-religious theme to the exclusion, almost, of all else. But that was not the only factor at work, nor the one which prevailed in the country to which Kierkegaard owed his intellectual formation. In Germany, the eighteenth century was not irreligious in tone; it was the age of poetry rather than of prose, and as such discovered a new world. The period of the *Aufklärung* was not so much the end of a phase as the beginning of a new age which declared itself in the Romantic renaissance, one element of which was the religious revival. For while at first rationalism appeared to make the divorce between religion and culture absolute, the revolution could not be halted and led to a reversal of the trend which had begun three hundred years earlier. Religion and culture, it is true, were distinguished and delimited as formerly they were not—but the very fact of being thus distinguished revealed a new relationship between them: no longer taken for granted and imposed by tradition, but personal and free.

This turning point in the history of the *Aufklärung* as it merges into the Romantic renaissance, can be pinpointed in the pages of Immanuel Kant, whose answer to the question *What is Enlightenment?* shows how the rationalistic separation of thought and existence ended by pointing towards an existentialist synthesis—in the same way that the separation of religion and culture prepared the way for their reunion in the religious revival which followed.

Enlightenment, Kant writes, is the emergence of man from a childhood of which he himself is guilty. To be a minor means to be incapable of using one's understanding without being directed by another. That minority is one's own fault when it is due not to lack of understanding, but to lack of decision and of the courage to act independently. *Sapere aude!* Have the courage to use your understanding! is the motto of the *Aufklärung*.

The correspondence which Kant establishes between emancipation and responsibility was to be the crux of the philosophical revolution: the parting of the ways. One answer was idealism, another positivism, as in Hegel and Marx; but the third way, the middle way, led to a personalist and existentialist answer, already prominent in Fichte, and which Kierkegaard was the first to give methodically

in a form consistent with Christianity—
until Maurice Blondel published *L'Action* in
1893.[1]

But while Kant may be said to have set the
terms of the problem for the next generation,
it was his friend and neighbour in Königsberg,
Johann Georg Hamann, who was the secret
instigator of the Romantic movement and the
religious revival borne within it. In book xii of
Dichtung und Wahrheit, speaking of his intention
to edit Hamann's works, Goethe sums up the

[1] Kierkegaard's thought has been assimilated so persistently
to the schools of Protestant theology which it was instrumental
in provoking that it is time to stress other and no less fruitful
affinities, and in particular its parallels with one of the main
trends of Catholic thought. In English-speaking countries
Catholic philosophy is usually regarded as inevitably taking
the form of Thomism or Scholasticism. This is not true of
France or of Germany. For this reason it will not be out of
place to observe that the father of modern Catholic philosophy
(and this might be extended to include theology), Blondel,
writing without knowledge of Kierkegaard's work, inaugurated an apologetic which is strikingly similar to Kierkegaard's. With his starting point in Kant, his goal ' *l'option
religeuse* ' (the choice) and his description of the aesthetic
stage, Blondel parallels Kierkegaard. Seen in the company
of Blondel, Kierkegaard can moreover be seen from the
outside, and from a point of view which stresses the elements
in his work which habit tends to pass over. The rational
character of Kierkegaard's argument is thrown into relief
instead of a wearisome insistence on the ' paradox '. Blondel,
Laberthonière, Louis Lavelle and Le Senne, like Gabriel
Marcel, may owe little or nothing to Kierkegaard, but the
parallels are only more impressive. Examples among Anglican
and Catholic writers in England are not wanting, and I might
mention Langmead Casserley's *The Christian in Philosophy* and
Illtyd Trethowan's *An Essay in Christian Philosophy* (published
by Faber and Longman's respectively).

source of Hamann's influence and points to the problem which his work raised—so accurately that it is tempting to think that Kierkegaard (whom little escaped) was first sent to the obscure Hamann and his own problem from this unlikely source.

The principle to which all Hamann's statements lead back is this: " Everything a man does, whether in action, or word or otherwise, must spring from the united power of all his faculties: everything isolated is to be rejected." A splendid maxim! but difficult to carry out. It is, no doubt, applicable in life and in art; but when it comes to transmitting something by the word, and if the word is not poetic, a great difficulty arises. For the word must detach itself and become isolated in order to say and to mean something. In speaking a man must, for the moment, be one-sided; there can be no communication, no teaching, without particularisation.

Goethe's brief reference to Hamann defines the problem analysed at such length in the *Unscientific Postscript* where Kierkegaard attempts to establish harmony between the two forms of communication, the direct and the indirect. ' Thought,' he writes, ' may well despise imagination; but *en revanche* imagination despises thought, and the same is true

of feeling. The task is not to annul the one at
the expense of the other, but on the contrary
to preserve their equilibrium, their simultaneity; and the plane on which they are
united is *existence*.'[1]

Kierkegaard, then, proceeds to examine the
present age in the light of Kant's motto, and of
Hamann's 'splendid maxim', and like
Diogenes, he takes his lantern and goes in
search of the honest man, the individual. What
he observes is grouped under four main head-
ings with which he characterises the present
age: as the age of reflection; of 'the many'
and the levelling process; of the individual
self-consciously distinct from the herd; and
finally as the age in which authority assumes a
new importance. But the sign of the times is
'reflection', the heightened self-consciousness
through which 'the age' has to pass on attaining its majority, a danger but also a challenge
which cannot be avoided. The view which he
puts forward was common to a number of
writers of the period, and when Sainte-Beuve
paused to consider his own circumstances in
1832, in the light of Lamennais' warnings, he
reached the same conclusions.

The rarest of things is assuredly the moral
energy of the will. The eighteenth century
certainly possessed a powerful one and in

[1] This 'task' is discussed briefly in the Introduction to
the Torchbook edition (Harper) of *Kierkegaard's Journals*.

spite of its contradictions and inconsistencies, deployed it in the field of revolt and exhausted it in feats of destruction . . . Among those who devote themselves to thought, and whose domain is that of the moral sciences and philosophy, nothing is more difficult to discover at the present time than a will at the heart of an intelligence, a conviction, a *faith* . . . People want to understand without believing, would like to receive ideas like a limpid mirror, without being determined thereby, I do not say to acts, but even to conclusions.

(*Portraits Contemporains*, Vol. I, 200)

Sainte-Beuve's diagnosis is not quoted as a confirmation of Kierkegaard's view so much as to help the reader to see him from outside, for the difficulty with much of Kierkegaard's thought lies in avoiding being drawn into his wake and drowned by the force of imagination. Sainte-Beuve is talking in the same terms as Kant and as Hamann, and adds, like Kierkegaard, that the emancipation of thought is all too rarely condensed into real knowledge by decision and action. The energy of the eighteenth century had been expressed in the optimism, no doubt facile at times, which led it to destroy the old régime in the full confidence that it could rebuild a new and better world in which man, no longer a minor, would be master of his fate. That was the driving power of the Enlightenment which worked itself out in the systems of Hegel and Marx, but ignored the individual. The immediate consequence of reflection without decision is, however, not only the levelling process taken in its social and political sense, but in its moral sense, when it becomes a threat to the very existence of the individual.

Like Sainte-Beuve, Kierkegaard begins at the point where the tension between emancipation and responsibility, between thought and existence gives a further significance to Kant's *sapere aude*—which Nietzsche was to translate as ' live dangerously!'. If reflection was not to drown in its own verbosity it must be anchored in life on pain of becoming isolated from the other faculties in man; and that could only happen if his thought, words and deeds were the expression of ' the united power of all his faculties ': of reason, will and feeling. But with the transition from a more naïve to a more reflective life, which constitutes the attainment of majority, that harmony is infinitely more difficult to achieve, and the danger is that feeling will lose caste and be looked upon with contempt. Then, what Kierkegaard indifferently calls pathos, feeling or enthusiasm is degraded to the rank of sentiment and emotion. Reflection lives in a world of quantity and calculation and cannot by itself penetrate into the realm of quality and decision. So that what the

present age most needs is strong and lucid
feeling, 'it needs pathos, just as scurvy needs
greens.'

At this point in his argument, Kierkegaard
forestalls one of the most famous passages in
Nietzsche. Reflection cannot, of course, stifle
feeling completely; but it can repress and
cripple it in a particular way. In a naïve age
passion is the spring of action released by the
will; in an age of reflection however, if it is
denied its natural function and remains
'unventilated', feeling does not merely
atrophy: it is poisoned. The form which it
then assumes is envy or, to use the expression
canonised by Nietzsche, *ressentiment*. [1] As Toc-

---

[1] *Ressentiment* is something more than envy or resentment,
and is currently used in German. Max Scheler has defined
its meaning in *L'Homme du Ressentiment* p. 9 (Gallimard):

'If I have used the word "ressentiment" it is not because
of any predilection for the French language but because there
is no equivalent in German (or, we might add, in English).
Moreover, Nietzsche has justified its use in a technical sense.
As far as I can see it has two meanings as used currently in
France: on the one hand the experience and the rumination
of a certain emotional reaction directed against another which
gives that feeling the power to grow deeper and gradually to
penetrate the very soul of the individual while entirely
renouncing the field of action and expression. That sort of
rumination, that continual revivifying of the feeling is therefore quite a different thing from a purely intellectual
recollection of that feeling and of the circumstances which
gave it birth. It is a revivifying of the emotion itself, a re-
sentiment. In the second place the word suggests a whole
world of negation and animosity. In that respect the German
word *Groll* (ill-will) well expresses that hidden, continuously

queville noted at the same time, the feeling behind the levelling process is envy, and the fewer the privileges the more they are resented. But envy does not only transform the political and social world; it grows into a moral ressentiment (p. 53) and secretly, almost unconsciously, dictates the scale of moral values. Here Kierkegaard discusses *ressentiment* in much the same terms as Nietzsche in *The Genealogy of Morals* and *Beyond Good and Evil;* though where Nietzsche traces the genealogy of 'the slave morality' to Christianity, Kierkegaard regards it as belonging to the age of reflection, as the danger to which Sainte-Beuve draws attention.

All these factors taken together—the characteristics of reflection, the levelling process, the situation of the individual, and the general view which holds them together and gives them their special significance, the conviction that man had attained his majority—all combine to throw the question of authority into relief in a new manner. Antiquity and Christendom had each solved the question in their own way, naïvely or spontaneously, and therefore in a way which was no longer

---

grumbling exasperation which is independent of the activity of the self and which little by little engenders a ruminative hate, or an animosity without any definite object towards which it is hostile, but big with an infinite number of hostile intentions.'—

relevant (p. 57). Authority could no longer be
buttressed by extrinsic arguments, by an appeal
to tradition or to the Bible, but had to be
reached after passing through reflection, and
grasped in ' the choice.' In this light it
becomes ' the most important ethico-religious
concept ' and in a sense the central problem of
Kierkegaard's life and work—as may be seen
from the insistence with which he repeats that
he writes ' without authority '. For authority
is the mode in which ' the other ', the transcendent, enters into existence, the moment at
which ' the choice ' through being subjective,
through its inwardness, grasps the objective,
the transcendent. Christianity is radically
falsified unless it comes with authority, and
however orthodox the doctrine it remains
human and immanent unless preached with
authority. And here again Kant provides the
starting-point:

> Real self-reduplication (i.e. the reduplication
> of thought in existence) without a third
> factor, which is outside one and compels one,
> is an impossibility . . .

But Kant held that man was his own law
(autonomy), i.e. bound himself under the law
which he gave himself. In a deeper sense
that means lawlessness or experimentation.
It is no more severe than the thwacks which
Sancho Panza applied to his own bottom. I
can no more be really stricter as A than I am

or than I wish to be as B. There must be some compulsion.

It is perfectly true that if a man does not act decisively he can evade the issue, but once the full rigour of the moral law is invoked it cannot be arbitrarily interrupted, and he is led by the logic of his decision to the frontier of transcendence, to *l'option religieuse*, to the choice, to the recognition of an objective authority, the absolute. If reflection and emancipation is to involve a responsibility which is more than a subjective notion, it must submit to the exigencies of action. Up to a certain moment everything is seen and grasped as immanent, inherent in the unfolding of self-consciousness, but at that point it abuts upon authority. Authority is not a constraint upon reflection nor a limitation of freedom, but the goal revealed by their use.

In the first essay, authority is considered in relation to politics and morals. In the second Kierkegaard treats of it from the standpoint of Christianity. 'A genius and an apostle are qualitatively different, they are definitions which each belong in their own spheres: *the sphere of immanence, and the sphere of transcendence* ' (p. 105). Kierkegaard had begun by examining the case of Adler, but was soon speaking in general terms. And when he writes that a man is not called by revelation to sit back and enjoy his possessions undisturbed, he is referring to those who believe or behave as though Christianity were the product of " religious genius "— an expression which when applied to himself he dismissed as self-contradictory. An apostle does not possess the doctrine for his own sake, and he does not speak like a writer of genius or a poet for whom no " in order that " is involved; nor like a philosopher contemplating the truth for its own sake. ' He is, on the contrary, on a mission and has to proclaim the doctrine and use authority.' In Christendom there was no doubt a sense in which it was right and proper to enjoy undisturbed possession of the doctrine; but in the new situation in which Christianity found itself that could no longer be so, and both mission and authority, belonging together, appear in a new context. Only, of course, authority must not be confused with authority in the political and social sphere. It is certainly power, but spiritual power; not the power of the ' tyrant ' or a worldly sort of power, but the power of the ' martyr ' to compel others to attend. Kierkegaard did not confuse himself with the apostle, and regarded his mission to be to ' draw attention ' to Christianity ' without authority '. No doubt his personal dilemma and his position in Copenhagen sometimes make his attitude on the subject of authority appear ambiguous; but his statements are not: the doctrine must be proclaimed with authority, and the character of the priesthood is indelible.

The Bible has virtually been done away with, and indeed in Protestant countries it was just as necessary to attack the illusion that the Bible was authority as to attack the illusion of Christendom in order to make people think clearly. But he was only " a sort of poet-thinker " and his task was to draw attention to the fact that a consistent view of the immanent world of reflection reduplicated in existence, in action, led up to ' the choice ', to what Blondel calls ' *un saut de générosité au delà de la portée des justifications intellectuelles* '—to ' the leap of faith ', an act of generosity which the envy of the age of reflection always tends to stifle.

The error of traditional apologetics, the ' crumb of untruth ' which floats along in the wake of Christianity, and which Christendom, ' the establishment ', encouraged, was to minimize the risk, to play down the *sapere aude!* In the present age that error would be fatal; for it would be impossible to exaggerate the changes which had taken place upon a man's attaining his majority. Kierkegaard had nothing against traditional apologetics at the right time and in the right place. But the choice must come first. For it is through the choice that man becomes ' the individual ', and it is in the immanent sphere that he prepares himself for the transcendent. ' I bind myself to make every man whom I can include in the category " the

individual " into a Christian, or rather, since no
man can do that for another, I vouch for his
becoming one.' Man, in fact, ' only begins to
exist in faith ', though he must begin by
existing as ' the individual '. The ' choice ' is
the gateway to existence, the point at which
reflection and action intersect and are fused by
the passion which gives action its quality. To
explain that double movement, the equilibrium
between thought and feeling, Kierkegaard
writes that ' life must be lived forward and
understood backward.' That does not mean
moving blindly forward, but that action,
advancing in the light of reflection, throws a
fresh light backward and further qualifies and
clarifies reflection. In the present age that twofold form of reflection is the only one which
corresponds with the exigencies of the moral
and intellectual situation.

Up to the present [the conflict between
reflection and Christianity] has been between
reflection and simple, immediate [or naïve]
Christianity; from now on it will be between
reflection and simplicity armed with reflection . . . For behold! reflection performs the
opposite service by once again bringing the
springs of Christianity into play.

(Journals. 813)

At first it seemed as though the Enlightenment would abolish Christianity; but reflection
could not be halted, and completed the circle of

thought and brought the springs of Christianity into play by giving 'the choice' a new significance, by linking moral responsibility to the emancipation of thought in such a way that freedom calls to authority. In that sense the present age is also the age of the revival of Christianity, only that the revival or revivals which have marked the nineteenth century may not be regarded as leading to a situation in which the Church and the individual could sit back and enjoy possession of the doctrine, but to a situation in which the revival is endemic, and the accent falls upon the mission and upon authority. But authority nevertheless remains a scandal and an offence.

Divine authority is *the category* and here it is *the possibility of offence.* For a genius may well at one time or another, for fifty or a hundred years, shock *aesthetically*, but he can never be the cause of offence *ethically*, for the offence is that a man possesses divine authority.

The offence does not lie only or even primarily in the intellectual sphere, as though it were the *content* of revelation which reflection could in no circumstances accept. The cause of offence is the authority with which it must be proclaimed, the sign which marks the difference between the sphere of immanence and the sphere of transcendence. Reflection has not only brought the springs of Christianity into play, it has raised the price of faith which

can no longer be had as an adjunct to a cultural
tradition but must be bought by the individual.
The levelling process has done or is doing its
work; and ultimately leaves the individual
without support, either to sink and be lost in
the masses, ' the many ', or to be saved by the
transcendent. The conclusion of *The Present
Age* can perhaps be appreciated more fully by
comparing it to the conclusion of *Beyond Good
and Evil*.

> The complete degeneration of mankind to
> the level of what socialist fools and block-
> heads call ' the man of the future '—their
> ideal!—the degeneration and dwarfing of
> man into a herd animal, or as they say into
> the man of ' free society ', the brutalizing of
> man into a pigmy with equal rights and
> claims is undoubtedly *possible!* . . . And
> anyone who has thought out that possibility
> to the end will have experienced a new sense
> of disgust unknown to other men—and
> perhaps, too, a new *mission*.[1]

Kierkegaard's work became his mission
during the years when, looking *back* on what
he had written, he suddenly realised its
significance for the present age—which on a
different level he had always had in mind.
The revolutions of 1848 confirmed him in his
opinion. The changes taking place were

[1] (*Beyond Good and Evil, Complete Works*, Leipzig 1899, vol.
xii, 144).

transforming the situation in which Christianity had to be preached:

For the development is, in spite of everything, a progress because all the individuals who are saved will receive the specific weight of religion, its essence at first hand, from God himself. Then it will be said: behold, all is in readiness, see how the cruelty of abstraction makes the true form of worldliness only too evident, the abyss of eternity opens before you, the sharp scythe of the leveller makes it possible for everyone individually to leap over the blade—and behold, it is God who waits. Leap then into the arms of God!

THE PRESENT AGE

Our age is essentially one of understanding and reflection, without passion, momentarily bursting into enthusiasm, and shrewdly relapsing into repose.

If we had statistical tables of the consumption of intelligence from generation to generation as we have for spirits, we should be astounded at the enormous amount of scruple and deliberation consumed by small, well-to-do families living quietly, and at the amount which the young, and even children, use. For just as the children's crusade may be said to typify the Middle Ages, precocious children are typical of the present age. In fact one is tempted to ask whether there is a single man left ready, for once, to commit an outrageous folly.

Nowadays not even a suicide kills himself in desperation. Before taking the step he deliberates so long and so carefully that he literally chokes with thought. It is even questionable whether he ought to be called a suicide, since it is really thought which takes his life. He does not die *with* deliberation but *from* deliberation.

It would therefore be very difficult to prosecute the present generation in view of its

legal quibbles: in fact, its ability, virtuosity and
good sense consists in trying to reach a judgement and a decision without ever going as far
as action. If one may say of the revolutionary
period that it runs wild, one would have to say
of the present that it runs badly. Between them,
the individual and his generation always bring
each other to a standstill, with the result that
the prosecuting attorney would find it next to
impossible to get any fact admitted—because
nothing really happens. To judge from in-
numerable indications, one would conclude
that something quite exceptional had either just
happened or was just about to happen. Yet any
such conclusion would be quite wrong. Indications are, indeed, the only achievements of the
age; and its skill and inventiveness in con-
structing fascinating illusions, its bursts of
enthusiasm, using as a deceitful escape some
projected change of form, must be rated as
high in the scale of cleverness and of the
negative use of strength as the passionate,
creative energy of the revolution in the corresponding scale of energy. But the present
generation, wearied by its chimerical efforts,
relapses into complete indolence. Its condition
is that of a man who has only fallen asleep
towards morning: first of all come great
dreams, then a feeling of laziness, and finally a
witty or clever excuse for remaining in bed.

However well-meaning and strong the individual man may be (if he could only use his strength), he still has not the passion to be able to tear himself from the coils and seductive uncertainty of reflection. Nor do his surroundings supply the events or produce the general enthusiasm necessary in order to free him. Instead of coming to his help, his *milieu* forms around him a negative intellectual opposition, which juggles for a moment with a deceptive prospect, only to deceive him in the end by pointing to a brilliant way out of the difficulty —by showing him that the shrewdest thing of all is to do nothing. For at the bottom of the tergiversation of the present age is *vis inertiae*, and every one without passion congratulates himself upon being the first to discover it, and so becomes cleverer still. During the revolution arms were distributed freely, just as during the Crusades the insignia of the exploit were bestowed upon men, but nowadays people are supplied with rules of careful conduct and ready-reckoners to facilitate judgement. If a generation were given the diplomatic task of postponing any action in such a way as to make it seem as if something were just about to happen, then we should have to admit that our age had performed as remarkable a feat as the revolutionary age. Let any one try forgetting all he knows of the age and its actual relativity which is so enhanced by familiarity, and then arrive, as it were, from another world: if he

were then to read a book or an article in the
papers, or merely to speak to some passer-by,
his impression would be: ' Good heavens,
something is going to happen to-night—or perhaps something happened the night before last.'

A revolutionary age is an age of action; ours
is the age of advertisement and publicity. Nothing ever happens but there is immediate
publicity everywhere. In the present age a
rebellion is, of all things, the most unthinkable.
Such an expression of strength would seem
ridiculous to the calculating intelligence of our
times. On the other hand a political virtuoso
might bring off a feat almost as remarkable.
He might write a manifesto suggesting a general
assembly at which people should decide upon a
rebellion, and it would be so carefully worded
that even the censor would let it pass. At the
meeting itself he would be able to create the
impression that his audience had rebelled, after
which they would all go quietly home—having
spent a very pleasant evening. Among the
young men of to-day a profound and pro-
digious learning is almost unthinkable; they
would find it ridiculous. On the other hand a
scientific virtuoso might draw up a sub-
scription form outlining an all-embracing
system which he purposed to write and, what
is more, in such a way that the reader would
feel he had already read the system; for the
age of encyclopaedists, when men wrote

gigantic folios with unremitting pains, is gone. Now is the turn of those light-weight encyclopaedists who, *en passant*, deal with all the sciences and the whole of existence. Equally unthinkable among the young men of to-day is a truly religious renunciation of the world, adhered to with daily self-denial. On the other hand almost any theological student is capable of something far more wonderful. He could found a society with the sole object of saving all those who are lost. The age of great and good actions is past, the present is the age of anticipation when even recognition is received in advance. No one is satisfied with doing something definite, every one wants to feel flattered by reflection with the illusion of having discovered at the very least a new continent. Like a young man who decides to work for his examination in all earnest from September 1st, and in order to strengthen his resolution decides to take a holiday during August, so the present generation seems—though this is decidedly more difficult to understand—to have made a solemn resolution that the next generation should set to work seriously, and in order to avoid disturbing or delaying the next generation, the present attends to—the banquets. Only there is a difference: the young man understands himself in the light-heartedness of youth, whereas our generation is serious—even at banquets.

There is no more action or decision in our day than there is perilous delight in swimming in shallow waters. But just as a grown-up, struggling delightedly in the waves, calls to those younger than himself: ' Come on, jump in quickly '—the decision in existence, so to speak (of course it is in the individual), calls out to the young who are not as yet worn out by over-reflective thought or overburdened by the illusions of reflective thought: Come on, leap cheerfully, even if it means a light-hearted leap, so long as it is decisive. If you are capable of being a man, then danger and the harsh judgement of existence on your thoughtlessness will help you to become one.

If the jewel which every one desired to possess lay far out on a frozen lake where the ice was very thin, watched over by the danger of death, while, closer in, the ice was perfectly safe, then in a passionate age the crowds would applaud the courage of the man who ventured out, they would tremble for him and with him in the danger of his decisive action, they would grieve over him if he were drowned, they would make a god of him if he secured the prize. But in an age without passion, in a reflective age, it would be otherwise. People would think each other clever in agreeing that it was unreasonable and not even worth while to venture so far out. And in this way they would transform *daring and enthusiasm* into a *feat of skill*, so as to do something, for after all 'something must be done.' The crowds would go out to watch from a safe place, and with the eyes of connoisseurs appraise the accomplished skater who could skate almost to the very edge (i.e. as far as the ice was still safe and the danger had not yet begun) and then turn back. The most accomplished skater would manage to go out to the furthermost point and then perform a still more dangerous-looking run, so as to make the spectators hold their breath and say: 'Ye Gods! How mad; he is risking his life.' But look, and you will see that his skill was so astonishing that he managed to turn back just in time, while the ice was perfectly safe and there was still no danger. As at the theatre, the crowd would applaud and acclaim him, surge homeward with the heroic artist in their midst, to honour him with a magnificent banquet. For intelligence has got the upper hand to such an extent that it transforms the real task into an unreal trick and reality into a play. During the banquet admiration would reach its height. Now the proper relation between the admirer and the object of admiration is one in which the admirer is edified by the thought that he is a man like the hero, humbled by the thought that he is incapable of such great actions, yet morally encouraged to emulate him according to his powers; but where intelligence has got the upper hand the character of admiration is completely altered. Even at the height of the banquet, when the applause was loudest, the admiring guests would all have a shrewd notion that the action of the man who received all the honour was not really so extraordinary, and that only by chance was the gathering for him, since after all, with a little practice, every one could have done as much. Briefly, instead of being strengthened in their discernment and encouraged to do good, the guests would more probably go home with an even stronger predisposition to the most dangerous, if also the most respectable, of all diseases: to admire in public what is considered unimportant in private—since everything is made into a joke. And so, stimulated by a gush of admiration, they are all comfortably agreed that they might just as well admire themselves.

Formerly it was agreed that a man stood or fell by his actions; nowadays, on the contrary, every one idles about and comes off brilliantly with the help of a little reflection, knowing perfectly well what ought to be done. But what two people talking together, or the speakers at a meeting, understand perfectly presented to them as a thought or as an observation, they cannot understand at all in the form of action. If some one were to overhear what people said ought to be done, and then in a spirit of irony, and for no other reason, proceeded to act accordingly, every one would be amazed. They would find it rash, yet as soon as they had talked it over they would find that it was just what should be done.

The present age with its sudden enthusiasms followed by apathy and indolence is very near the comic; but those who understand the comic see quite clearly that the comic is not where the present age imagines. Now satire, if it is to do a little good and not cause immeasurable harm, must be firmly based upon a consistent ethical view of life, a natural distinction which renounces the success of the moment; otherwise the cure will be infinitely worse than the disease. The really comic thing is that an age such as this should try to be witty and humorous; for that is most certainly the last and most acrobatic way out of the impasse. What, indeed, is there for an age of reflection and thought to defy with humour? For, being without passion, it has lost all feeling for the values of eros, for enthusiasm and sincerity in politics and religion, or for piety, admiration and domesticity in everyday life. But even if the vulgar laugh, life only mocks at the wit which knows no values. To be witty without possessing the riches of inwardness is like squandering money upon luxuries and dispensing with necessities, or, as the proverb says, like selling one's breeches to buy a wig. But an age without passion has no values, and everything is transformed into representational ideas. Thus there are certain remarks and expressions current which, though true and reasonable up to a point, are lifeless. On the other hand no hero, no lover, no thinker, no knight of the faith, no proud man, no man in despair would claim to have experienced them completely and personally. And just as one longs for the clink of real money after the crackle of bank-notes, one longs nowadays for a little originality. Yet what is more spontaneous than wit? It is more spontaneous, at least more surprising, even than the first bud of spring and the first tender shoots of grain. Why, even if spring came according to agreement it would still be spring, but wit upon agreement would be disgusting.

But, now, supposing that as a relief from feverish and sudden enthusiasms things went so far that wit, that divine accident—an additional favour which comes as a sign from the gods, from the mysterious source of the inexplicable, so that not even the wittiest of men dares to say: to-morrow, but adoringly says: when it pleases the gods—but supposing that wit were to be transformed into its shabbiest contrary, a trivial necessity, so that it became a profitable branch of trade to manufacture and make up and remake, and buy up old and new witticisms—what an epigram on a witty age!

In the end, therefore, money will be the one thing people will desire, which is moreover only representative, an abstraction. Nowadays a young man hardly envies anyone his gifts, his art, the love of a beautiful girl, or his fame; he only envies him his money. Give me money, he will say, and I am saved. But the young man will not run riot, he will not deserve what repentance repays. He would die with nothing to reproach himself with, and under the impression that if only he had had the money he might really have lived and might even have achieved something great.

After these general observations, and having compared the present age with the revolutionary age, it will be in order to go back to the dialectical and categorical definitions of the present age, regardless whether they are present at a given moment or not. We are concerned here with the 'how' of the age, and this 'how' must be defined from a universal standpoint, the final consequences of which can be reached by deduction, *a posse ad esse*, and verified by observation and experience *ab esse ad posse*.

As far as its significance is concerned it is, of course, possible that the work of reflection, which is the task before the present age, may ultimately be explained in a higher form of existence. As for its quality, there is no doubt that the individual resting in his reflection can be just as well-intentioned as a passionate man

who has made his decision; and conversely
there may be just as much excuse for the man
whose passions run away with him as for a man
whose fault is never apparent, though he is
cleverly aware that he lets himself be deceived
by his reflection. The results of reflection are
both dangerous and unforeseeable because one
can never tell whether the decision which saves
a man from evil is reached after thorough consideration, or whether it is simply the exhaus-
tion resulting from reflection which prevents
him from doing wrong. One thing, however,
is certain, an increased power of reflection like
an increased knowledge only adds to man's
affliction, and above all it is certain that for the
individual as for the generation no task is more
difficult than to escape from the temptations of
reflection, simply because they are so dialectical
and the result of one clever discovery may give
the whole question a new turn, because at any
moment reflection is capable of explaining
everything quite differently and allowing one
some way of escape; because at the last
moment of a reflective decision reflection is
capable of changing everything—after one has
made far greater exertions than are necessary
to get a man of character into the midst of
things.

But these are only the excuses of reflection
and the real position in reflection remains
unchanged, for it is only altered *within* reflec-

tion. Even if a certain injustice is done to the present age when it is compared to a complete and closed period (the present age is still struggling with all the difficulties of ' becoming '), such a qualification is only a reflective qualification; and then, in return, its uncertainty is filled with *hope*.

A passionate tumultuous age will *overthrow everything, pull everything down;* but a revolutionary age, that is at the same time reflective and passionless, transforms that expression of strength into *a feat of dialectics: it leaves everything standing but cunningly empties it of significance. Instead of culminating in a rebellion it reduces the inward reality of all relationships to a reflective tension which leaves everything standing but makes the whole of life ambiguous: so that everything continues to exist factually whilst by a dialectical deceit,* privatissime, *it supplies a secret interpretation—that it does not exist.*

Morality is character, character is that which is engraved (χαράσσοω); but the sand and the sea have no character and neither has abstract intelligence, for character is really inwardness. Immorality, as energy, is also character; but to be neither moral nor immoral is merely ambiguous, and ambiguity enters into life when the qualitative distinctions are weakened by a gnawing reflection. The revolt of the passions is elemental, the dissolution brought about by ambiguity is a silent sorites[1] that goes on night and day. The distinction between good and evil is enervated by a superficial, superior and theoretical knowledge of evil, and by a supercilious cleverness which is aware that goodness is neither appreciated nor worth while in this world, that it is tantamount to stupidity. No one is any longer carried away by the desire for the good to perform great things, no one is precipitated by evil into atrocious sins, and so there is nothing for either the good or the bad to talk about, and yet for that very reason people gossip all the more, since ambiguity is tremendously stimulating and much more verbose than rejoicing over goodness or repentance over evil.

The springs of life, which are only what they are because of the qualitative differentiating power of passion, lose their elasticity. The distance separating a thing from its opposite in quality no longer regulates the inward relation of things. All inwardness is lost, and to that extent the relation no longer exists, or else forms a colourless cohesion. The negative law is this: opposites are unable to dispense with each other and unable to hold together. The positive law is that they are able to dispense with each other and are able to hold together or, stated positively: opposites are unable to dispense with

[1] A form of sophism leading by gradual steps from truth to absurdity.—Tr.

each other because of the connexion between
them. But when the inward relation is wanting
another takes its place: a quality is no longer
related to its contrary; instead, the partners
both stand and observe each other and *the state
of tension thus produced is really the end of the
relationship*. For example, the admirer no longer
cheerfully and happily acknowledges greatness,
promptly expressing his appreciation, and then
rebelling against its pride and arrogance. Nor
is the relationship in any sense the opposite.
The admirer and the object of admiration stand
like two polite equals, and observe each other.
A subject no longer freely honours his king or is
angered at his ambition. To be a subject has
come to mean something quite different; it
means to be a *third party*. The subject ceases
to have a position within the relationship; he
has no direct relation to the king but simply
becomes an observer and deliberately works out
the problem; i.e. the relation of a subject to
his king. For a time committee after committee
is formed, so long, that is to say, as there are
still people who passionately want to be what
they ought to be; but in the end the whole
age becomes a committee. A father no longer
curses his son in anger, using all his parental
authority, nor does a son defy his father, a
conflict which might end in the inwardness of
forgiveness; on the contrary, their relationship
is irreproachable, for it is really in process of

ceasing to exist, since they are no longer related
to one another within the relationship; in fact
it has become a problem in which the two
partners observe each other as in a game,
instead of having any relation to each other, and
they note down each other's remarks instead of
showing a firm devotion. More and more
people renounce the quiet and modest tasks of
life, that are so important and pleasing to God,
in order to achieve something greater; in order
to think over the relationships of life in a higher
relationship till in the end the whole generation
has become a representation, who represent . . .
it is difficult to say *who;* and who think about
these relationships . . . for *whose* sake it is not
easy to discover. A disobedient youth is no
longer in fear of his schoolmaster—the relation
is rather one of indifference in which schoolmaster and pupil discuss how a good school
should be run. To go to school no longer
means to be in fear of the master, or merely to
learn, but rather implies being interested in the
problem of education. Again the differentiating
relation of man to woman is never broken in
an audaciously licentious manner; decency is
observed in such a way that one can only
describe these innocent borderline flirtations as
trivial.

What in fact should one call such relationships? A tension, I think, is the best description, not, however, a tension which strains the

forces to breaking-point, but rather a tension which exhausts life itself and the fire of that enthusiasm and inwardness which makes the fetters of dependance and the crown of dominion light, which makes the child's obedience and the father's authority joyful, the admiration of the subject and the exaltation of the great fearless, which gives recognized importance to the master and thus to the disciple occasion to learn, which unites woman's weakness and man's strength in the equal strength of devotion. As it is the relationships still exist but they lack the force which makes it possible for them to draw together in inwardness and unite in harmony. The relationship expresses its presence and its absence simultaneously, not completely but rather as though it were drawled out, half-awake and uninterruptedly.

Perhaps I can explain what I mean by a very simple illustration? I once knew a family who owned a grandfather clock whose works for some reason or other had got out of order. But the fault did not result in the spring suddenly unwinding, or in the chain breaking or in the hand ceasing to strike; on the contrary, it went on striking in a curiously abstract, though confusing, way. It did not strike twelve times at twelve o'clock and once at one o'clock, but struck once all through the day at regular intervals. It went on striking all day long but never gave a definite time.

The same applies to a state of exhausted tension: the relationship continues; something is expressed with an abstract continuity which prevents any real break, but although it must nevertheless be described as an expression of the relationship, the relationship is not only ambiguously expressed, it is almost meaningless.

It is this deceptive lull in the relationship which continues the relation as a fact; the danger is that it favours the cunning deprivations of reflection. Against a rebellion one can use force, and an obvious counterfeit has only to wait for its punishment; but dialectical complications are difficult to root out, and it requires even better ears to track down the stealthy movement of reflection along its secret and ambiguous path.

The established order of things continues to exist, but it is its ambiguity which satisfies our reflective and passionless age. No one, for example, wishes to do away with the power of the king, but if little by little it could be transformed into something purely fictitious every one would be quite prepared to cheer him. No one, for example, wishes to bring about the downfall of the eminent, but if distinction could be shown to be purely fictitious then every one would be prepared to admire it. In the same way people are quite prepared to leave the Christian terminology untouched, but they can surreptitiously interpolate that it involves no decisive thought. And so they remain unrepentant, for after all they have destroyed nothing. They no more desire a powerful king than an heroic liberator or religious authority. In all innocence they want the established order to continue, but they have the more or less certain reflective knowledge that it no longer exists. Then they proudly imagine that their attitude is ironical—as though real irony were not essentially a concealed enthusiasm in a negative age (just as the hero is enthusiasm made manifest in a positive age), as though irony did not involve sacrifice, when its greatest master was put to death.

This reflective tension ultimately constitutes itself into a principle, and just as in a passionate age *enthusiasm* is the unifying principle, so in an age which is very reflective and passionless *envy* is the negative unifying principle. This must not, however, be interpreted as an ethical charge; the idea of reflection is, if one may so express it, envy, and it is therefore twofold in its action: it is selfish within the individual and it results in the selfishness of the society around him, which thus works against him.

The envy in reflection (within the individual) prevents him making a decision passionately.

If, for a moment, it should seem as though an
individual were about to succeed in throwing off
the yoke of reflection, he is at once pulled up by
the opposition of the reflection which surrounds
him. The envy which springs from reflection
imprisons man's will and his strength. First of
all the individual has to break loose from the
bonds of his own reflection, but even then he is
not free. Instead he finds himself in the vast
prison formed by the reflection of those around
him, for because of his relation to his own
reflection he also has a certain relation to the
reflection around him. He can only escape
from this second imprisonment through the
inwardness of religion, no matter how clearly
he may perceive the falseness of the situation.
With every means in its power reflection
prevents people from realizing that both the
individual and the age are thus imprisoned, not
imprisoned by tyrants or priests or nobles or the
secret police, but by reflection itself, and it does
so by maintaining the flattering and conceited
notion that the *possibility* of reflection is far
superior to a mere *decision*. A selfish envy makes
such demands upon the individual that by
asking too much it prevents him from doing
anything. It spoils him like an indulgent
mother, for the envy within him prevents the
individual from devoting himself to others.
Moreover, the envy which surrounds him
and in which he participates by envying

others, is envious in a negative and critical sense.

But the further it is carried the more clearly does the envy of reflection become a moral *ressentiment*. Just as air in a sealed space becomes poisonous, so the imprisonment of reflection develops a culpable *ressentiment* if it is not ventilated by action or incident of any kind. In reflection the state of strain (or tension as we called it) results in the neutralization of all the higher powers, and all that is low and despicable comes to the fore, its very impudence giving the spurious effect of strength, while protected by its very baseness it avoids attracting the attention of *ressentiment*.

It is a fundamental truth of human nature that man is incapable of remaining permanently on the heights, of continuing to admire anything. Human nature needs variety. Even in the most enthusiastic ages people have always liked to joke enviously about their superiors. That is perfectly in order and is entirely justifiable so long as after having laughed at the great they can once more look upon them with admiration; otherwise the game is not worth the candle. In that way *ressentiment* finds an outlet even in an enthusiastic age. And as long as an age, even though less enthusiastic, has the strength to give *ressentiment* its proper character and has made up its mind what its expression signifies, *ressentiment* has its own,

though dangerous, importance. In Greece, for
example, the form *ressentiment* took was ostracism, a self-defensive effort, as it were, on the
part of the masses to preserve their equilibrium
in face of the outstanding qualities of the
eminent. The outstanding man was exiled, but
every one understood how dialectical the
relationship was, ostracism being a mark of
distinction. Thus, in representing a somewhat
earlier period in the spirit of Aristophanes, it
would be more ironical to let a completely
unimportant person be ostracized than to let
him become dictator, because ostracism is the
negative mark of greatness. But it would be still
better to let the story end with the people
recalling the man whom they had ostracized
because they could no longer do without him,
and he would then be a complete mystery to the
country of his exile, which would, of course, be
quite unable to discover anything remarkable
about him. In *The Knights* Aristophanes gives
us a picture of the final state of corruption in
which the vulgar rabble ends when—just as in
Tibet they worship the Dalai Lama's excre-
ment—they contemplate their own scum in its
representatives; and that, in a democracy, is a
degree of corruption comparable to auctioning
the crown in a monarchy. But as long as
ressentiment still has any character, ostracism is a
negative mark of distinction. The man who
told Aristides that he had voted for his exile

' because he could not endure hearing Aristides called the only just man ' did not deny Aristides' eminence, but admitted something about himself. He admitted that his relation to distinction was the unhappy love of envy, instead of the happy love of admiration, but he did not try to belittle that distinction.

On the other side, the more reflection gets the upper hand and thus makes people indolent, the more dangerous *ressentiment* becomes, because it no longer has sufficient character to make it conscious of its significance. Bereft of that character reflection is cowardly and vacillating, and according to circumstances interprets the same thing in a variety of ways. It tries to treat it as a joke, and if that fails, to regard it as an insult, and when that fails, to dismiss it as nothing at all; or else it will treat the thing as a witticism, and if that fails then say that it was meant as a moral satire deserving attention, and if that does not succeed, add that it is not worth bothering about.

Thus *ressentiment* becomes the constituent principle of want of character, which from utter wretchedness tries to sneak itself a position, all the time safeguarding itself by conceding that it is less than nothing. The *ressentiment* which results from want of character can never understand that eminent distinction really is distinction. Neither does it understand itself by recognizing distinction negatively (as in the case of ostracism) but wants to drag it down, wants to belittle it so that it really ceases to be distinguished. And *ressentiment* not only defends itself against all *existing* forms of distinction but against that which is still *to come*.

The *ressentiment* which is *establishing itself* is the process of levelling, and while a passionate age storms ahead setting up new things and tearing down old, raising and demolishing as it goes, a reflective and passionless age does exactly the contrary: it *hinders and stifles* all action; it levels. Levelling is a silent, mathematical, and abstract occupation which shuns upheavals. In a burst of momentary enthusiasm people might, in their despondency, even long for a misfortune in order to feel the powers of life, but the apathy which follows is no more helped by a disturbance than an engineer levelling a piece of land. At its most violent a rebellion is like a volcanic eruption and drowns every other sound. At its maximum the levelling process is a deathly silence in which one can hear one's heart beat, a silence which nothing can pierce, in which everything is engulfed, powerless to resist. One man can be at the head of a rebellion, but no one can be at the head of the levelling process alone, for in that case he would be the leader and would thus escape being levelled. Each individual within his own little circle can co-operate in the levelling, but it is an abstract power, and the levelling process is the victory of abstraction over the individual. The levelling process in modern times, corresponds, in reflection, to fate in antiquity.

The dialectic of antiquity tended towards leadership (the great individual and the masses —the free man and the slaves); so far the dialectic of Christendom tends towards representation (the majority sees itself in its representative and is set free by the consciousness that it is the majority which is represented, in a sort of self-consciousness); the dialectic of the present age tends towards equality, and its most logical—though mistaken—fulfilment is levelling, as the negative unity of the negative reciprocity of all individuals.

It must be obvious to every one that the profound significance of the levelling process lies in the fact that it means the predominance of the category ' generation ' over the category ' individuality'. In antiquity the total number of the individuals was there to express, as it were, the value of the outstanding individual. Nowadays the standard of value has been changed so that *equally*, approximately so and so many men go to one individual, and one need only be sure of having the right number in order to have importance. In antiquity the individual in the masses had no importance whatsoever; the outstanding individual signified them all. The present age tends towards a mathematical equality in which equally in all classes approximately so and so many people go to one individual. Formerly the outstanding individual could allow himself everything and the individual in the masses nothing at all. Now everyone knows that so and so many make an individual and quite consistently people add themselves together (it is called joining together, but that is only a polite euphemism) for the most trivial purposes. Simply in order to put a passing whim into practice a few people add themselves together, and the thing is done— then they dare do it. For that reason not even a pre-eminently gifted man can free himself from reflection, because he very soon becomes conscious of himself as a fractional part in some quite trivial matter, and so fails to achieve the infinite freedom of religion. The fact that several people united together have the courage to meet death does not nowadays mean that each, individually, has the courage, for, even more than death, the individual fears the judgement and protest of reflection upon his wishing to risk something on his own. The individual no longer belongs to God, to himself, to his beloved, to his art or to his science, he is conscious of belonging in all things to an abstraction to which he is subjected by reflection, just as a serf belongs to an estate. That is why people band together in cases where it is an absolute contradiction to be more than one. The apotheosis of the positive principle of association is nowadays the devouring and demoralizing principle which in the slavery of reflection makes even virtues into *vitia splendida*. There is no other reason for this than that eternal responsibility, and the religious singling out of the individual before God, is ignored. When corruption sets in at that point people seek consolation in company, and so reflection catches the individual for life. And those who do not realize even the beginning of this crisis are engulfed without further ado in the reflective relationship.

The levelling process is not the action of an individual but the work of reflection in the hands of an abstract power. It is therefore possible to calculate the law governing it in the same way that one calculates the diagonal in a parallelogram of forces. The individual who levels down is himself engulfed in the process and so on, and while he seems to know selfishly what he is doing one can only say of people *en masse* that they know not what they do; for just as collective enthusiasm produces a surplus which does not come from the individual, there is also a surplus in this case. A demon is called up over whom no individual has any power, and though the very abstraction of levelling gives the individual a momentary, selfish kind of enjoyment, he is at the same time signing the warrant for his own doom. Enthusiasm *may* end in disaster, but levelling is *eo ipso* the destruction of the individual. No age, and therefore not the present age, can bring the scepticism of that process to a halt, for as soon as it tries to stop it, the law of the levelling process is again called into action. It can therefore only be held up by the individual attaining the religious courage which springs from his individual religious isolation.

I was once the witness of a street fight in which three men most shamefully set upon a fourth. The crowd stood and watched them with indignation; expressions of disgust began to enliven the scene; then several of the on-lookers set on one of the three assailants and knocked him down and beat him. The avengers had, in fact, applied precisely the same rules as the offenders. If I may be allowed to do so, I will introduce my own unimportant self into the story and continue. I went up to one of the avengers and tried by argument to explain to him how illogical his behaviour was; but it seemed quite impossible for him to discuss the question: he could only repeat that such a rascal richly deserved to have three people against him. The humour of the situation would have been even more apparent to some one who had not seen the beginning of the brawl, and so simply heard one man saying of another (who was alone) that he was three against one, and heard the remark just when the very reverse was the case—when they were three to one against him. In the first place it was humorous because of the contradiction which it involved, as when the policeman told a man standing in the street ' to kindly disperse '. Secondly it had all the humour of self-contradiction. But what I learnt from it was that I had better give up all hope of putting a stop to that scepticism, lest it should turn upon me.

No single individual (I mean no outstanding individual—in the sense of leadership and conceived according to the dialectical category ' fate ') will be able to arrest the abstract process of levelling, for it is negatively something higher, and the age of chivalry is gone. No society or association can arrest that abstract power, simply because an association is itself in the service of the levelling process. Not even the individuality of the different nationalities can arrest it, for on a higher plane the abstract process of levelling is a negative representation of *humanity pure and unalloyed*. The abstract levelling process, that self-combustion of the human race, produced by the friction which arises when the individual ceases to exist as singled out by religion, is bound to continue, like a trade wind, and consume everything. But through it each individual for himself may receive once more a religious education and, in the highest sense, will be helped by the *examen rigorosum* of the levelling process to an essentially religious attitude. For the younger men who, however strongly they personally may cling to what they admire as eminent, realize from the beginning that the levelling process is evil in both the selfish individual and in the selfish generation, but that it can also, if they desire it honestly and before God, become the starting-point for the highest life—for them it will indeed be an education to live in the age of levelling. Their age will, in the very highest sense, develop them religiously and at the same time educate them aesthetically and intellectually, because in this way the comic will receive its absolute expression. The highest form of the comic arises precisely when the individual comes directly under the infinite abstraction of ' pure humanity ', without any of those intermediary qualifications which temper the humour of man's position and strengthen its pathos, without any of the concrete particulars of organization which the levelling process destroys. But that again is only another expression of the fact that man's only salvation lies in the reality of religion for each individual.

And it will add fuel to their enthusiasm to understand that it is in fact through error that the individual is given access to the highest, if he courageously desires it. But the levelling process will have to continue, and must be completed, just as the scandal had to come into the world, though woe to them by whom it comes.

It has often been said that a reformation should begin with each man reforming himself. That, however, is not what actually happened, for the reformation produced a hero who paid God dearly enough for his position as hero. By joining up with him directly people buy cheap, indeed at bargain prices, what he had paid for so dearly; but they do not buy the highest of all things. The abstract principle of levelling, on the contrary, like the biting east wind, has no personal relation to any individual but has only an abstract relationship which is the same for every one. There, no hero suffers for others, or helps them; the taskmaster of all alike is the levelling process which itself takes on their education. And the man who learns most from the levelling and himself becomes greatest does not become an outstanding man or a hero— that would only impede the levelling process, which is rigidly consistent to the end—he himself prevents that from happening because he has understood the meaning of levelling; he becomes a man and nothing else, in the complete equalitarian sense. That is the idea of religion. But, under those conditions, the equalitarian order is severe and the profit is seemingly very small; seemingly, for unless the individual learns in the reality of religion and before God to be content with himself, and learns, instead of dominating others, to dominate himself, content as priest to be his own audience, and as author his own reader, if he will not learn to be satisfied with that as the highest, because it is the expression of the equality of all men before God and of our likeness to others, then he will not escape from reflection. It may be that for one deceptive moment it will seem to him, in relation to his gifts, as though he were levelling, but in the end he will sink down beneath the levelling process. There is no good calling upon a Holger Danske or a Martin Luther; their day is over and at bottom it is only the individual's laziness which makes a man long to have them back, a worldly impatience which prefers to buy something cheap, second-hand, rather than to buy the highest of all things very dear and first-hand. It is worse than useless to found society after society, because negatively speaking there is something above them, even though the short-sighted member of the society cannot see it.

The principle of individuality in its *immediate* and beautiful formation is symbolized for the generation in the outstanding and eminent individual; it groups subordinate individualities round the representative. This principle of individuality, in its *eternal* truth, uses the abstraction and equality of the generation to level down, and in that way co-operates in developing the individual religiously into a real man. For the levelling process is as powerful where temporary things are concerned as it is impotent where eternal things are concerned. Reflection is a snare in which one is caught, but, once the 'leap' of enthusiasm has been taken, the relation is a different one and it becomes a noose which drags one into eternity. Reflection is and remains the hardest creditor in existence; hitherto it has cunningly bought up all the possible views of life, but it cannot buy the essentially religious and eternal view of life; on the other hand, it can tempt people astray with its dazzling brilliance, and dishearten them by reminding them of all the past. But, by leaping into the depths, one learns to help oneself, learns to love others as much as oneself, even though one is accused of arrogance and pride— because one will not accept help—or of selfishness, because one will not cunningly deceive people by helping them, i.e. by helping them to escape their highest destiny.

Should any one complain that what I have set forth here is known to all and could be said by any one, then my answer is: the more the merrier—I am not asking for a position of eminence and I have nothing against every one knowing my opinion, unless that were to mean, in a sense, that it is to be taken from me and thereby put at the disposal of a negative association. So long as I have permission to

c

retain them, my opinions do not lose their
value by being known to every one.

Throughout many changes the tendency in
modern times has remained a levelling one.
These changes themselves have not, however,
all of them, been levelling, for they are none of
them abstract enough, each having a certain
concrete reality. To some extent it is true that
the levelling process goes on when one great
man attacks another, so that both are weakened,
or when one is neutralized by the other, or
when an association of people, in themselves
weak, grow stronger than the eminent. Levelling can also be accomplished by one particular
caste, e.g. the clergy, the bourgeois, the
peasants, by the people themselves. But all
that is only the first movement of an abstract
power within the concreteness of individuality.

In order that everything should be reduced
to the same level, it is first of all necessary to
procure a phantom, its spirit, a monstrous
abstraction, an all-embracing something which
is nothing, a mirage—and that phantom is *the
public*. It is only in an age which is without
passion, yet reflective, that such a phantom can
develop itself with the help of the Press which
itself becomes an abstraction. In times of
passion and tumult and enthusiasm, even when
a people desire to realize a fruitless idea and lay

waste and destroy everything: even then there is no such thing as a public. There are parties and they are concrete. The Press, in times such as those, takes on a concrete character according to the division of parties. But just as sedentary professional people are the first to take up any fantastic illusion which comes their way, so a passionless, sedentary, reflective age, in which only the Press exhibits a vague sort of life, fosters this phantom. The public is, in fact, the real Levelling-Master rather than the actual leveller, for whenever levelling is only approximately accomplished it is done by something, but the public is a monstrous nothing. The public is a concept which could not have occurred in antiquity because the people *en masse*, *in corpore*, took part in any situation which arose, and were responsible for the actions of the individual, and, moreover, the individual was personally present and had to submit at once to applause or disapproval for his decision. Only when the sense of association in society is no longer strong enough to give life to concrete realities is the Press able to create that abstraction ' the public ', consisting of unreal individuals who never are and never can be united in an actual situation or organization—and yet are held together as a whole.

The public is a host, more numerous than all the peoples together, but it is a body which can never be reviewed, it cannot even be repres-

ented, because it is an abstraction. Nevertheless, when the age is reflective and passionless
and destroys everything concrete, the public
becomes everything and is supposed to include everything. And that again shows
how the individual is thrown back upon
himself.

The real moment in time and the real
situation being simultaneous with real people,
each of whom is something: that is what helps
to sustain the individual. But the existence of
a public produces neither a situation nor simultaneity. The individual reader of the Press is
not the public, and even though little by little a
number of individuals or even all of them
should read it, the simultaneity is lacking.
Years might be spent gathering the public
together, and still it would not be there. This
abstraction, which the individuals so illogically
form, quite rightly repulses the individual
instead of coming to his help. The man who
has no opinion of an event at the actual
moment accepts the opinion of the majority,
or, if he is quarrelsome, of the minority. But
it must be remembered that both majority and
minority are real people, and that is why the
individual is assisted by adhering to them. A
public, on the contrary, is an abstraction. To
adopt the opinion of this or that man means
that one knows that they will be subjected to the
same dangers as oneself, that they will be led

astray with one if the opinion leads astray. But to adopt the same opinion as the public is a deceptive consolation because the public is only there *in abstracto*. Whilst, therefore, no majority has ever been so certain of being right and victorious as the public, that is not much consolation to the individual, for a public is a phantom which forbids all personal contact. And if a man adopts public opinion to-day and is hissed to-morrow he is hissed by the public.

A generation, a people, an assembly of the people, a meeting or a man, are responsible for what they are and can be made ashamed if they are inconstant and unfaithful; but a public remains a public. A people, an assembly or a man can change to such an extent that one may say: they are no longer the same; a public on the other hand can become the very opposite and still be the same—a public. But it is precisely by means of this abstraction and this abstract discipline that the individual will be formed (in so far as the individual is not already formed by his inner life), if he does not succumb in the process, taught to be content, in the highest religious sense, with himself and his relation to God, to be at one with himself instead of being in agreement with a public which destroys everything that is relative, concrete and particular in life; educated to find peace within himself and with God, instead of counting hands. And the ultimate difference between the modern world and antiquity is: that ' the whole ' is not concrete and is therefore unable to support the individual, or to educate him as the concrete should (though without developing him absolutely), but is an abstraction which by its abstract equality repels him and thus helps him to be educated absolutely—unless he succumbs in the process. The *taedium vitae* so constant in antiquity was due to the fact that the outstanding individual was what others *could not be;* the inspiration of modern times will be that any man who finds himself, religiously speaking, has only achieved what *every one can achieve.*

A public is neither a nation, nor a generation, nor a community, nor a society, nor these particular men, for all these are only what they are through the concrete; no single person who belongs to the public makes a real commitment; for some hours of the day, perhaps, he belongs to the public—at moments when he is nothing else, since when he really is what he is he does not form part of the public. Made up of such individuals, of individuals at the moments when they are nothing, a public is a kind of gigantic something, an abstract and deserted void which is everything and nothing. But on this basis any one can arrogate to himself a public, and just as the Roman Church chimerically extended its frontiers by appointing bishops *in partibus infidelium,* so a public is something which every one can claim, and even a drunken sailor exhibiting a 'peep-show' has dialectically absolutely the same right to a public as the greatest man; he has just as logical a right to put all those many noughts *in front* of his single number.

A public is everything and nothing, the most dangerous of all powers and the most insignificant: one can speak to a whole nation in the name of the public, and still the public will be less than a single real man, however unimportant. The qualification 'public' is produced by the deceptive juggling of an age of reflection, which makes it appear flattering to the individual who in this way can arrogate to himself this monster, in comparison with which concrete realities seem poor. The public is the fairy story of an age of understanding, which in imagination makes the individual into something even greater than a king above his people [1]; but the public is also a gruesome abstraction through which the individual will receive his religious formation—or sink.

The Press is an abstraction (since a paper is

[1] As an author I have fortunately never sought for or had a public, but have contented myself with 'the individual', and on account of that limitation have almost become a proverb.

[All Kierkegaard's religious discourses, which form a large part of his works were dedicated to '"that individual"', whom with joy and thankfulness I call my reader because he reads, not thinking of the author, but of God'.]

not a concrete part of a nation and only in an abstract sense an individual) which in conjunction with the passionless and reflective character of the age produces that abstract phantom: a public which in its turn is really the levelling power. Consequently it has an importance apart from its negative religious importance.

The fewer ideas there are at any time, the more indolent and exhausted by bursts of enthusiasm will it be; nevertheless, if we imagine the Press growing weaker and weaker because no events or ideas catch hold of the age, the more easily will the process of levelling become a harmful pleasure, a form of sensual intoxication which flames up for a moment, simply making the evil worse and the conditions of salvation more difficult and the probability of decline more certain. Although the demoralization brought about by autocracy and the decay of revolutionary periods have often been described, the decay of an age without passion is something just as harmful, though, on account of its ambiguity, it is less obvious.

It may not be without interest to consider this point. More and more individuals, owing to their bloodless indolence, will aspire to be nothing at all—in order to become the public: that abstract whole formed in the most ludicrous way, by all participants becoming a third party (an onlooker). This indolent mass which understands nothing and does nothing itself, this gallery, is on the look-out for distraction and soon abandons itself to the idea that everything that any one does is done in order to give it (the public) something to gossip about. That indolent mass sits with its legs crossed, wearing an air of superiority, and any-one who tries to work, whether king, official, school-teacher or the better type of journalist, the poet or the artist, has to struggle to drag the public along with it, while the public thinks in its own superior way that it is the horse.

If I tried to imagine the public as a particular person (for although some better individuals momentarily belong to the public they never-theless have something concrete about them, which holds them in its grip even if they have not attained the supreme religious attitude), I should perhaps think of one of the Roman emperors, a large well-fed figure, suffering from boredom, looking only for the sensual intox-ication of laughter, since the divine gift of wit is not earthly enough. And so for a change he wanders about, indolent rather than bad, but with a negative desire to dominate. Every one who has read the classical authors knows how many things a Caesar could try out in order to kill time. In the same way the public keeps a dog to amuse it. That dog is the scum of the

literary world.[1] If there is some one superior to
the rest, perhaps even a great man, the dog is
set on him and the fun begins. The dog goes for
him, snapping and tearing at his coat-tails,
allowing itself every possible ill-mannered
familiarity—until the public tires, and says it
may stop. That is an example of how the public
levels. Their betters and superiors in strength
are mishandled—and the dog remains a dog
which even the public despises. The levelling is
therefore done by a third party; a non-
existent public levelling with the help of a third
party which in its insignificance is less than
nothing, being already more than levelled. And
so the public is unrepentant, for it was after all
not the public that acted but the dog; just as
one says to children—the cat's mother did it.
The public is unrepentant—it was not really
belittling any one; it just wanted a little amuse-
ment. For had the levelling implement been
remarkably energetic, the indolent public
would have been fooled because the implement
itself would have been in the way; but when
their betters are held down by the insignificant
and the insignificant by itself, then no one is
quit of anything.

The public is unrepentant, for it is not they
who own the dog—they only subscribe. They
neither set the dog on any one, nor whistle it off

[1] *The Corsair,* the paper in which Kierkegaard was lam-
pooned.

—directly. If asked they would answer: the dog is not mine, it has no master. And if the dog had to be killed they would say: it was really a good thing that bad-tempered dog was put down, every one wanted it killed—even the subscribers.

Perhaps some one, familiarizing himself with such a case, and inclined to fix his attention upon the outstanding individual who suffered at the hands of the public, may be of the opinion that such an ordeal is a great misfortune. I cannot at all agree with such an opinion, for any one who really wishes to be helped to attain the highest is in fact benefited by undergoing such a misfortune, and must rather desire it even though people may be led to rebel. The really terrible thing is the thought of all the lives that are or easily may be wasted. I will not even mention those who are lost, or at any rate led completely astray: those who play the part of the dog for money, but the many who are helpless, thoughtless and sensual, who live superior lazy lives and never receive any deeper impression of existence than this meaningless grin, and all those bad people who are led into further temptation because in their stupidity they even become self-important by com- miserating with the one who is attacked, with- out even understanding that in such a position the person attacked is always the stronger, without understanding that in this case the terrible and ironical truth applies: Weep not over him but over yourselves.

That is the levelling process at its lowest, for it always equates itself to the divisor by means of which every one is reduced to a common denominator. Eternal life is also a sort of levelling, and yet that is not so, because the common denominator is that every one should really and essentially be a man in a religious sense.

Hitherto I have been dealing with the dialectical categories and qualifications, and with their consequences, whether actually present at any given moment or not. I shall now abandon the dialectical analysis of the present age in order to arrive dialectically at its concrete affirmations regarding everyday life. It is here that the darker side will be seen; but although this cannot be denied, it is equally certain that just as reflection itself is not evil, so a very reflective age has its lighter side, simply because a higher degree of reflection implies greater significance than immediate passion; for when enthusiasm intervenes to gather the powers of reflection together into a decision, and because reflection confers, on the average, a greater capacity for action—then, when religion enters in, it takes command of that increased capacity for action.

Reflection is not the evil; but a reflective

condition and the deadlock which it involves, by transforming the capacity for action into a means of escape from action, is both corrupt and dangerous, and leads in the end to a retrograde movement.

The present age is essentially one of understanding lacking in passion, and has therefore abolished the *principle of contradiction*. By comparison with a passionate age, an age without passion gains in *scope what it loses in intensity*. But this scope may once again become the condition of a still higher form, if a corresponding intensity assumes control of the extended field of activity which is put at its disposal. The abolition of the principle of contradiction, expressed in terms of existence, means to live in contradiction with oneself. The creative omnipotence of the differentiating power of passion, which makes the individual completely at one with himself, is transformed into the extended scope of reflective understanding: as a result of knowing and being everything possible, one is in contradiction with oneself, i.e. nothing at all. The principle of contradiction strengthens the individual's faithfulness to himself and makes him as constant as the number three spoken of so beautifully by Socrates, when he says that it would rather endure anything than become four or even a large round number, and in the same way the individual would

rather suffer and be true to himself than be
all manner of things in contradiction with
himself.

What is *talkativeness*? It is the result of doing
away with the vital distinction between talking
and keeping silent. Only some one who knows
how to remain essentially silent can really talk
—and act essentially. Silence is the essence of
inwardness, of the inner life. Mere gossip antici-
pates real talk, and to express what is still in
thought weakens action by forestalling it. But
some one who can really talk, because he knows
how to remain silent, will not talk about a
variety of things but about one thing only, and
he will know when to talk and when to remain
silent. Where mere scope is concerned, talkativeness wins the day, it jabbers on incessantly
about everything and nothing. When people's
attention is no longer turned inwards, when
they are no longer satisfied with their own inner
religious lives, but turn to others and to things
outside themselves, where the relation is
intellectual, in search of that satisfaction, when
nothing important ever happens to gather the
threads of life together with the finality of a
catastrophe: that is the time for talkativeness.
In a passionate age great events (for they
correspond to each other) give people something to talk about. Talkativeness, on the
contrary, has, in quite another sense, plenty to

talk about. And when the event is over, and silence follows, there is still something to remember and to think about while one remains silent. But talkativeness is afraid of the silence which reveals its emptiness.

The law governing artistic production applies, on a smaller scale, to every one in daily life. Every man who has a real experience experiences at the same time all its possibilities in an ideal sense, including the opposite possibility. Aesthetically these possibilities are his lawful property. Not so, however, his private and personal reality. His talk and his production both rest upon his silence. The ideal perfection of his talk and of his production will correspond to his silence, and the absolute expression of that silence will be that the ideal will include the qualitatively opposite possibility. But as soon as the artist prostitutes his own reality he is no longer essentially productive. His beginning is his end, and his very first word will be a sin against the modesty of the ideal. This type of artistic production is therefore even, aesthetically speaking, a kind of private gossip. It is easily recognized because it is not balanced by its opposite; for ideality is the balance of opposites. For example, if the man who is moved to write by suffering is really initiated into the realm of ideals, he will reproduce the happiness as well as the suffering of his experience with the same affection. The condition of

his attaining this ideal is the silence with which
he shuts off his own real personality. Otherwise, in spite of all precautions, such as changing the scene to Africa, his one-sided predilection will be privately recognizable. For an
author, like any one else, must have his own
private personality, but it must be his own
$\overset{\text{'}}{\alpha}\delta\upsilon\tau o\nu$[1]; and just as the entrance to a house is
barred by the crossed bayonets of the guards,
the approach to a man's personality is barred
by the dialectical cross of qualitative opposites
in an ideal equilibrium.

What is true of the greater relationship and is
very clear in the above circumstances, which is
why they were instanced, is also true in a lesser
degree of the smaller ones; and, once again,
silence is the *conditio sine qua non* of all educated
social intercourse. The more thoroughly a man
grasps the ideal and the idea—in silence—the
more capable will he be of reproducing man's
daily life so that it seems as though he only
talked of particular things at a certain distance.
The less ideal, the more superficial his talk, and
his conversation will become a meaningless
repetition of names, of ' absolutely reliable '
private information of what this and that
person—mentioning all their names—had said,
&c. &c., and conversation in general will take
on a talkative confidential note about what one
is doing or going to do, what one would have

[1] Holy of Holies.

said on a certain occasion, which particular girl one is making love to, why nevertheless one does not want to marry. The introspection of silence is the condition of all educated social intercourse; the exteriorized caricature of inwardness is vulgarity and talkativeness.

One finds excellent examples of the kind of talkativeness I am referring to in the novel.[1] It consists entirely of trivialities, people's names are always mentioned and they are people whose trivial way of life is interesting because of their names. People who are talkative certainly chatter away about something and, indeed, their one wish is to have an excuse for more gossip, but the subject is non-existent from the ideal point of view. It always consists of some trivial fact such as that Mr. Madsen is engaged and has given his fiancée a Persian shawl; that Petersen, the poet, is going to write some new poems, or that Marcussen, the actor, mispronounced a certain word last night. If we could suppose for a moment that there was a law which did not forbid people talking, but simply ordered that everything which was spoken about should be treated as though it had happened fifty years ago, the gossips would be done for, they would be in despair. On the other hand, it would not really interfere with any one who could really talk. That an actor should have mispronounced a word could only

[1] Which Kierkegaard was reviewing: *The Two Ages*.

be interesting if there was something interesting
in the mispronunciation itself, in which case the
fifty years make no difference—but Miss Gusta,
for example, would be in despair, she who had
been at the theatre that very evening, in a box
with Alderman Waller's wife; for was it not *she*
who noticed the slip and even noticed a member
of the chorus smiling, &c. &c. It really would
be a shame and cruelty to all those silly gossip-
ing people who must all the same be allowed to
live—and so the law is only posited.

With gossip, therefore, the vital distinction
between what is private and what is public is
obliterated, and everything is reduced to a kind
of private-public gossip which corresponds more
or less to the public of which it forms part. The
public is public opinion which interests itself in
the most private concerns. Something that nobody would dare to tell to a gathering, that
nobody could *talk* about, and which even the
gossips would not like to admit to having
gossiped about, can perfectly well be written
for the public and, as a member of the public,
people may know all about it.

What is *formlessness*? It is the result of doing
away with the vital distinction between form
and content. Formlessness may, therefore,
unlike madness or stupidity, have a content
that is true, but the truth it contains can never
be essentially true. It will be capable of being

extended so as to include everything or touch upon everything, whereas a real content is clearly, and, if one likes, miserably limited because of its intensity and self-absorption.

The universality of formlessness in a passionless but reflective age is expressed, moreover, not only by the fact that the most varied ideas are found dallying in the same company but by the diametrically opposite fact that people find a paramount longing for and pleasure in 'acting on principle'. A principle, as the word indicates, is what comes first, i.e. the substance, the idea in the undeveloped form of feeling and of enthusiasm which drives on the individual by its own inner power. That is entirely wanting in a passionless individual. To him a principle is something purely external for the sake of which he does one thing as willingly as another, and the opposite of both into the bargain. The life of an individual without passion is not the development of a self-revealing principle. On the contrary, his inner life is something hurrying along, always on the move and always hurrying to do something ' on principle '. A principle, in that sense, becomes a monstrous something or other, an abstraction, just like the public. And while the public is something or other so monstrous that not all the nations of the world and all the souls in eternity put together are as numerous, every one, even a drunken sailor, can have a public, and the

same is true of ' a principle '. It is something
immense which even the most insignificant
man can add to the most insignificant action,
and thus become tremendously self-important.
When an honest insignificant man suddenly
becomes a hero for the sake of a principle, the
result is quite as comic as though fashion
decreed that every one was to wear a cap with a
peak thirty feet long. If a man had a little
button sewn on the inner pocket of his coat ' on
principle ' his otherwise unimportant and quite
serviceable action would become charged with
importance—it is not improbable that it would
result in the formation of a society.

It is acting ' on principle ' which does away
with the vital distinction which constitutes
decency. For decency is immediate (whether
the immediateness is original or acquired). It
has its seat in feeling and in the impulse and
consistency of an inner enthusiasm. ' On principle ' one can do anything and what one does
is, fundamentally, a matter of indifference, just
as a man's life remains insignificant even though
' on principle ' he gives his support to all the
' needs of the times ', even when, by virtue of
being a mute and in that capacity as ' the organ
of public opinion ' he is as well known as the
figures on a barrel-organ that can move forward
and bow, plate in hand. ' On principle ' a man
can do anything, take part in anything and himself remain inhuman and indeterminate. ' On

principle' a man may interest himself in the
founding of a brothel (there are plenty of social
studies on the subject written by the health
authorities), and the same man can ' on principle ' assist in the publication of a new Hymn
Book because it is supposed to be the great need
of the times. But it would be as unjustifiable
to conclude from the first fact that he was de-
bauched as it would, perhaps, be to conclude
from the second that he read or sang hymns. In
this way everything becomes permissible if done
' on principle '. The police can go to certain
places on ' official duty ' to which no one else
can go, but as a result one cannot deduce anything from their presence. In the same way one
can do anything ' on principle ' and avoid all
personal responsibility. People pull to pieces
' on principle ' what they admire personally,
which is nonsensical, for while it is true that
everything creative is latently polemical, since
it has to make room for the new which it is
bringing into the world, a purely destructive
process is nothing and its principle is emptiness
—so what does it need space for? But modesty,
repentance and responsibility cannot easily
strike root in ground where everything is done
' on principle '.

What is *superficiality* and the desire to show
off? Superficiality is the result of doing away
with the vital distinction between concealment

and manifestation. It is the manifestation of emptiness, but where mere scope is concerned it wins, because it has the advantage of dazzling people with its brilliant shams. Real manifestation is homogeneous, because it is really profound, whereas superficiality has a varied and *omnium gatherum* appearance. Its love of showing off is the self-admiration of conceit in reflection. The concealment and reserve of inwardness is not given time in which to conceive an essential mystery, which can then be made manifest, but is disturbed long before that time comes and so, as a reward, reflection attracts the gaze of egotism upon its varied shams whenever possible.

What is *flirtation*? It is the result of doing away with the vital distinction between real love and real debauchery. Neither the real lover nor the real debauchee are guilty of flirting. A flirtation only toys with the possibility and is therefore a form of indulgence which dares to touch evil and fails to realize the good. To act ' on principle ' is also a kind of flirtation, because it reduces moral action to an abstraction. But in mere scope flirtation has all the advantages, for one can flirt with anything, but one can only really love *one* girl. From the point of view of love, properly understood, any addition is really a subtraction (even though in a confused age a capricious man may be blinded by pleasure), and the more one adds the more one takes away.

What is *reasoning?* It is the result of doing away with the vital distinction which separates subjectivity and objectivity. As a form of abstract thought reasoning is not profoundly dialectical enough; as an opinion and a conviction it lacks full-blooded individuality. But where mere scope is concerned, reasoning has all the apparent advantage; for a thinker can encompass his science, a man can have an opinion upon a particular subject and a conviction as a result of a certain view of life, but one can reason about anything.

In our own day anonymity has acquired a far more pregnant significance than is perhaps realized: it has an almost epigrammatic significance. People not only write anonymously, they sign their anonymous works: they even talk anonymously. The very soul of a writer should go into his style, and a man puts his whole personality into the style of his conversation, though limited by the exception which Matthias Claudius noted when he said that if any one conjured a book its *esprit* should appear—unless there was no *esprit* in it. Nowadays one can talk with any one, and it must be admitted that people's opinions are exceedingly sensible, yet the conversation leaves one with

the impression of having talked to an anonymity. The same person will say the most con-
tradictory things and, with the utmost calm,
make a remark, which coming from him is a
bitter satire on his own life. The remark itself
may be sensible enough, and of the kind that
sounds well at a meeting, and may serve in a
discussion preliminary to coming to a decision,
in much the same way that paper is made out
of rags. But all these opinions put together do
not make one human, personal opinion such as
you may hear from quite a simple man who
talks about very little but really does talk.
People's remarks are so objective, so all-
inclusive, that it is a matter of complete indifference who expresses them, and where human
speech is concerned that is the same as acting
' on principle '. And so our talk becomes like
the public, a pure abstraction. There is no
longer any one who knows how to talk, and instead, objective thought produces an atmos-
phere, an abstract sound, which makes human
speech superfluous, just as machinery makes
man superfluous. In Germany they even have
phrase-books for the use of lovers, and it will
end with lovers sitting together talking anonymously. In fact there are hand-books for everything, and very soon education, all the world
over, will consist in learning a greater or lesser
number of comments by heart, and people will
excel according to their capacity for singling

out the various facts like a printer singling out the letters, but completely ignorant of the meaning of anything.

Thus our own age is essentially one of understanding, and on the average, perhaps, more knowledgeable than any former generation, but it is without passion. Every one knows a great deal, we all know which way we ought to go and all the different ways we can go, but nobody is willing to move. If at last some one were to overcome the reflection within him and happened to act, then immediately thousands of reflections would form an outward obstacle. Only a proposal to reconsider a plan is greeted with enthusiasm; action is met by indolence. Some of the superior and self-satisfied find the enthusiasm of the man who tried to act ridiculous, others are envious because he made a beginning when, after all, they *knew* just as well as he did what should be done—but did not do it. Still others use the fact that some one has acted in order to produce numerous critical observations and give vent to a store of arguments, demonstrating how much more sensibly the thing could have been done; others again, busy themselves guessing the outcome and, if possible, influencing events a little so as to favour their own hypothesis.

It is said that two English noblemen were once riding along a road when they met a man whose horse had run away with him and who,

being in danger of falling off, shouted for help.
One of the Englishmen turned to the other
and said, ' A hundred guineas he falls off.'
' Taken,' said the other. With that they spurred
their horses to a gallop and hurried on ahead to
open the toll-gates and to prevent anything
from getting in the way of the runaway horse.
In the same way, though without that heroic
and millionaire-like spleen, our own reflective
and sensible age is like a curious, critical and
worldly-wise person who, at the most, has
vitality enough to lay a wager.

Life's existential tasks have lost the interest of
reality; illusion cannot build a sanctuary for the
divine growth of inwardness which ripens to
decisions. One man is curious about another,
every one is undecided, and their way of escape
is to say that some one must come who will do
something—and then they will bet on him.

It is quite impossible for the community or
the idea of association to save our age. On the
contrary, association is the scepticism, which is
necessary in order that the development of individuality may proceed uniformly, so that the
individual will either be lost or, disciplined by
such abstractions, will find himself religiously.
Nowadays the principle of association (which at
the most is only valid where material interests
are concerned) is not positive but negative; it
is an escape, a distraction and an illusion. Dialectically the position is this: the principle of

association, by strengthening the individual, enervates him; it strengthens numerically, but ethically that is a weakening. It is only after the individual has acquired an ethical outlook, in face of the whole world, that there can be any suggestion of really joining together. Otherwise the association of individuals who are in themselves weak, is just as disgusting and as harmful as the marriage of children.

Formerly the sovereign and the great each had their opinion and the rest were satisfied and decided enough to realize that they dared not or could not have an opinion. Now every one can have an opinion; but they have to band together numerically in order to have one. Twenty-five signatures make the most frightful stupidity into an opinion, and the considered opinion of a first-class mind is only a paradox. But when the context is meaningless it is useless to take a broad survey. The best that can be done is to consider each part of speech by itself. And if only nonsense comes out of a man's mouth it is useless to try and make a coherent speech, and it is better to take each word separately—and so with individuals.

The change which will come about is this. In the old order (which sprang from the relation between the individual and the generation) the officers, generals, heroes (i.e. the man of distinction, the leader within his own sphere) were *recognizable*, and every one (in proportion to his

authority), with his little detachment, fitted pic-
turesquely and organically into the whole, both
supporting and supported by the whole. From
now on the great man, the leader (according to
his position) will be without authority because
he will have divinely understood the diabolical
principle of the levelling process; he will be
unrecognizable; he will keep his distinction
hidden like a plain-clothes policeman, and his
support will only be negative, i.e. repelling
people, whereas the infinite indifference of
abstraction judges every individual and
examines him in his isolation. This order is dialectically the very opposite of that of the
Prophets and Judges, and just as the danger for
them lay in their authority not being recognized,
so nowadays the unrecognizable is in danger of
being recognized, and of being persuaded to
accept recognition and importance as an
authority, which could only hinder the highest
development. For they are unrecognizable and
go about their work like secret agents, not
because of any private instruction from God!
—for that is the case of Prophets and Judges—
but are unrecognizable (without authority) because they have understood the universal in
equality before God, and, because they realize
this and their own responsibility every moment,
are thus prevented from being guilty of thought-
lessly realizing in an inconsistent form this
consistent perception. This order is dialectically

the opposite of the organizing order symbolized in the outstanding personality, which makes the generation into a support for the individual, whereas now, like an abstraction, the generation is negatively supported by the unrecognizable, and turns polemically against the individual— in order to save every single individual religiously.

And so when the generation, which itself desired to level and to be emancipated, to destroy authority and at the same time itself, has, through the scepticism of the principle association, started the hopeless forest fire of abstraction; when as a result of levelling with this scepticism, the generation has rid itself of the individual and of everything organic and concrete, and put in its place ' humanity ' and the numerical equality of man and man: when the generation has, for a moment, delighted in this unlimited panorama of abstract infinity, unrelieved by even the smallest eminence, undisturbed by even the slightest interest, a sea of desert; then the time has come for work to begin, for every individual must work for himself, each for himself. No longer can the individual, as in former times, turn to the great for help when he grows con-fused. That is past; he is either lost in the dizziness of unending abstraction or saved for ever in the reality of religion. Perhaps very many will cry out in despair, but it will not

help them—already it is too late. If it is true
that in former times authorities and powers
were misused and brought upon themselves
the nemesis of revolution, it was weakness and
impotence which, desiring to stand alone,
brought this final nemesis upon them. Nor
shall any of the unrecognizable presume to
help directly or to speak directly or to teach
directly at the head of the masses, in order to
direct their decisions, instead of giving his
negative support and so helping the individual
to make the decision which he himself has
reached; any other course would be the end of
him, because he would be indulging in the
short-sighted compassion of man, instead of
obeying the order of divinity, of an angry, yet
so merciful, divinity. For the development is, in
spite of everything, a progress because all the
individuals who are saved will receive the
specific weight of religion, its essence at first
hand, from God himself. Then it will be said:
' behold, all is in readiness, see how the cruelty
of abstraction makes the true form of worldliness only too evident, the abyss of eternity
opens before you, the sharp scythe of the
leveller makes it possible for every one individually to leap over the blade—and behold, it is
God who waits. Leap, then, into the arms of
God .' But the ' unrecognizable ' neither can
nor dares help man, not even his most faithful
disciple, his mother, or the girl for whom he

would gladly give his life: they must make the leap themselves, for God's love is not a second-hand gift. And yet the 'unrecognizable' (according to his degree) will have a double work compared with the 'outstanding' man (of the same degree), because he will not only have to work continuously, but at the same time labour to conceal his work.

But the desolate abstraction of the levelling process will always be continued by its servants, lest it should end with a return of the old order. The servants of the levelling process are the servants of the powers of evil, for levelling itself does not come from divinity and all good men will at times grieve over its desolation, but divinity allows it and desires to bring the highest into relation with the individual, i.e. with each and every man. The servants of the levelling process are known to him who is 'unrecognizable', but he dare not use either power or authority against them, for that would be to reverse the development, since it would become immediately apparent to a third person that the 'unrecognizable' was an authority, and in that way the third man would be prevented from attaining to the highest.

Only by suffering can the 'unrecognizable' dare to help on the levelling process and, by the same suffering action, judge the instruments. He dare not overcome the levelling process directly, that would be his end, for it would be the same as acting with authority. But he will overcome it in suffering, and in that way express once more the law of his existence, which is not to dominate, to guide, to lead, but to serve in suffering and help indirectly. Those who have not made the leap will look upon his unrecognizable action, his suffering as failure; those who have made the leap will suspect that it was victory, but they can have no certainty, for they could only be made certain by him, and if he gave that certainty to a single person it would be the end of him, because he would have been unfaithful to the divinity in desiring to play at being authority: that would mean that he had failed; not only by being unfaithful to God in trying to use authority, but because he did not obey God and teach men to love one another by compelling himself, so that even though they begged him to do so he should not have deceived them by exerting authority.

But I break off. All this is only fooling, for if it is true that every man must work for his own salvation, then all the prophecies about the future of the world are only valuable and allowable as a recreation, or a joke, like playing bowls or cards.

But it must always be remembered that reflection is not in itself something harmful, that, on the contrary, it is necessary to work through it in order that one's actions should be more intensive. The stages of all actions which are performed with enthusiasm are as follows: first of all comes immediate enthusiasm, then follows the stage of cleverness which, because immediate enthusiasm does not calculate, assumes with a calculating cleverness the appearance of being the higher; and finally comes the highest and most intensive enthusiasm which follows the stage of cleverness, and is therefore able to see the shrewdest plan of action but disdain it, and thereby receive the intensity of an eternal enthusiasm. For the time being, however, and for some time to come, this really intensive enthusiasm will remain completely misunderstood, and the question is whether it can ever become popular, i.e. whether one may presume upon such a degree of cleverness in the average man that cleverness will no longer seduce and enchant him, and may presume that he will be able to dominate it by having attained the highest form of enthusiasm, but as it were squander it—for an enthusiastic action, being always the opposite of shrewd, is never obvious. The enthusiasm of Socrates was not immediate. On the contrary, he was clever enough to see what he had to do in order to escape, although he disdained to act according to that opinion, just as he refused the proffered speech. That is why there is nothing obvious about his heroic death, and even in death he remained ironical by putting to the shrewd and

the clever the question whether he could really
have been clever, since he did the reverse. That
is the point at which cleverness is left hanging in
mid-air, hoist with its own reflective judgement and that of the world about it, afraid that
an action performed in the teeth of cleverness
may be confused with an action performed
without cleverness. An immediate enthusiasm
does not know such a danger, and therefore
requires the *impetus* of the most intense enthusiasm in order to get through life. Such an
enthusiasm is not mere rhetorical twaddle about
' high seriousness ', a still ' higher seriousness '
and an ' all highest seriousness '. It can be
known from its category: that it acts against
understanding. Neither does immediate goodness know the danger of reflection—where
goodness and weakness are mistaken and confused; and it is precisely for that reason that,
after reflection, it requires a religious *impetus* to
set goodness afloat again.

In our times, when so little is done, an extraordinary number of prophecies, apocalypses,
glances at and studies of the future appear, and
there is nothing to do but to join in and be one
with the rest. Yet I have the advantage over
the many who bear a heavy responsibility when
they prophesy and give warnings, because I can
be perfectly certain that no one would think of
believing me. So I do not ask that any one
should make a cross in their calendar or other-

wise bother to see whether my words are fulfilled. If they are fulfilled, then people will have something else to think about than my accidental being and if they are not fulfilled, well, then I shall simply be a prophet in the modern sense of the word—for a prophet now-adays means to prognosticate and nothing more. In a certain sense a prophet cannot do anything else. It was providence that fulfilled the words of the older prophets, so perhaps we modern prophets, lacking the addition coming from providence, might say with Thales: what we predict will either happen or not; for to us too has God granted the gift of prophecy.

OF THE DIFFERENCE
BETWEEN A GENIUS AND
AN APOSTLE

1847

What, exactly, have the errors[1] of exegesis and philosophy done in order to confuse Christianity, and how have they confused Christianity? Quite briefly and categorically, they have simply forced back the sphere of paradox-religion[2] into the sphere of aesthetics, and in consequence have succeeded in bringing Christian terminology to such a pass that terms which, so long as they remain within their sphere, are qualitative categories, can be put to almost any use as clever expressions. If the sphere of paradox-religion is abolished, or explained away in aesthetics, an Apostle becomes neither more nor less than a genius, and then—good night, Christianity! *Esprit* and the Spirit, revelation and originality, a call from God and genius, all end by meaning more or less the same thing.

That is how the errors of science[3] and learning have confused Christianity. The con-

[1] The errors, moreover, are not confined to heterodoxy but are also found in hyper-orthodoxy. They are in fact those of thoughtlessness.

[2] i.e. Christianity.

[3] S. K. does not mean the natural sciences. The word used is the same as the German *Wissenschaft*, which means science as a method. Occasionally I have used learning.—Tr.

fusion has spread from learning to the religious
discourse, with the result that one not in-
frequently hears priests, *bona fide*, in all learned
simplicity, prostituting Christianity. They talk
in exalted terms of St. Paul's brilliance and
profundity, of his beautiful similes and so on—
that is mere aestheticism. If St. Paul is to be
regarded as a genius, then things look black
for him, and only clerical ignorance would ever
dream of praising him in terms of aesthetics,
because it has no standard, but argues that all
is well so long as one says something good
about him. This kind of good-natured and
well-intentioned thoughtlessness is due to the
fact that the individual in question is not
disciplined by qualitative dialectic. If he were
he would have learnt that to say something
good of an apostle, when it is inapposite, does
him no service, for as a result he is acclaimed
for what in this case is a matter of indifference,
and admired as something which essentially he
is not, and then what he is is quite forgotten.
This kind of thoughtless eloquence is quite as
likely to celebrate St. Paul as a stylist and an
artist in words or, better still, since it is after
all well known that he was also engaged in a
craft, as a tent-maker whose masterly work
surpassed that of all upholsterers before and
since—for as long as one says something good
about St. Paul all is well. As a genius St. Paul
cannot be compared with either Plato or

Shakespeare, as a coiner of beautiful similes he comes pretty low down in the scale, as a stylist his name is quite obscure—and as an up-holsterer: well, I frankly admit I have no idea how to place him. The point is that it is always better to treat stupid solemnity as a joke and then the really serious thing becomes apparent, the fact that St. Paul is an Apostle. As an Apostle St. Paul has no connexion whatsoever with Plato or Shakespeare, with stylists or upholsterers, and none of them (Plato no more than Shakespeare or Harrison the upholsterer) can possibly be compared with him.

A genius and an apostle are qualitatively different, they are definitions which each belong in their own spheres; *the sphere of immanence, and the sphere of transcendence:*

(1) *Genius may, therefore, have something new to bring forth, but what it brings forth disappears again as it becomes assimilated by the human race, just as the difference ' genius ' disappears as soon as one thinks of eternity; the Apostle has, paradoxically, something new to bring, the newness of which, precisely because it is essentially paradoxical, and not an anticipation in relation to the development of the race, always remains, just as an Apostle remains an Apostle in all eternity, and no eternal immanence puts him on the same level as other men, because he is essentially, paradoxically different.* (2) *Genius is what it is of itself, i.e. through that which it is in itself; an Apostle is what he is by his divine authority.*

(3) Genius has only an immanent teleology; the Apostle is placed as absolute paradoxical teleology.

All thought breathes in immanence, whereas faith and the paradox are a qualitative sphere unto themselves. As between man and man, *qua* man, all differences are immanent, vanishing before essential and eternal thought, a factor which is certainly valid for the moment, but disappears in the essential equality of eternity. Genius is, as the word itself shows, immediateness (*ingenium*, that which is inborn, primative, *primus*, original, *origo*, &c.),[1] it is a natural qualification, genius *is born*. Even long before there can be any question as to how far genius is prepared to relate its particular gifts to God, it is genius, and it remains genius even if it does not do so. It is possible that genius may so change that it develops into what it is κάτα δύναμιν, so as to acquire conscious possession of itself. If one uses the expression 'paradox' in order to denote the something new which a genius may have to bring forth, it is only used in an inessential sense of the transitory paradox of the anticipation thus condensed into a paradox which, however, dis-

[1] *Genius* comes from the Latin *genius*, guardian spirit; but the word derives from the stem of the verb *gigno*, to give birth, and seems originally to have meant inherited power personified. Related to *genius* and *gigno* is *ingenium*, gift (from *in-gigno*, that is to say 'in-born'). S. K. is therefore right etymologically, though he did not know the root meaning of genius. (Note in the Danish edition S.V. XI, edited by A. B. Drachmann.)

appears again later. In his first communication
a genius may be paradoxical, but the more he
comes to himself, the more completely will the
paradox disappear. A genius may be a century
ahead of his time, and therefore appear to be a
paradox, but ultimately the race will assimilate
what was once a paradox in such a way that it is
no longer paradoxical.

It is otherwise with an Apostle. The word
itself indicates the difference. An Apostle is
not born; an Apostle is a man called and
appointed by God, receiving a mission from
him. An Apostle does not develop in such a
way that he successively becomes what he is
κάτα δύναμιν. For to become an Apostle is not
preceded by any potential possibility; essentially every man is equally near to becoming
one. An Apostle can never come to himself in
such a way that he becomes conscious of his
apostolic calling as a factor in the development
of his life. Apostolic calling is a paradoxical
factor, which from first to last in his life stands
paradoxically outside his personal identity with
himself as the definite person he is. A man
may perhaps have reached years of discretion
long ago, when suddenly he is called to be an
Apostle. As a result of this call he does not
become more intelligent, does not receive more
imagination, a greater acuteness of mind and so
on; on the contrary, he remains himself and by
that paradoxical fact he is sent on a particular

mission by God. By this paradoxical fact the
Apostle is made paradoxically different from all
other men for all eternity. The new which he
may have to bring forth is the essential paradox.
However long it may be proclaimed in the
world it remains essentially and equally new,
equally paradoxical, and no immanence can
assimilate it. The Apostle did not behave like
the man marked out by natural gifts who is
born before his time; he was perhaps what we
call a simple man, but by a paradoxical fact he
was called to proclaim this new thing. Even if
thought were to think that it could assimilate
the doctrine, it cannot assimilate the way in
which the doctrine came into the world; for the
essential paradox is the protest against immanence. But the way in which a doctrine of
this kind came into the world is qualitatively
decisive, and it can only be ignored by deceit
or by thoughtlessness.

(2) Genius is appreciated purely aesthetically,
according to the measure of its content, and its
specific weight; an Apostle is what he is through
having divine authority. *Divine authority is,
qualitatively, the decisive factor.* It is not by
evaluating the content of the doctrine aesthetically or intellectually that I should or could
reach the result: *ergo*, the man who proclaimed
the doctrine was called by a revelation; *ergo*,
he is an Apostle. The very reverse is the case:
the man who is called by a revelation and to

whom a doctrine is entrusted, argues from the fact that it is a revelation, from his authority. I have not got to listen to St. Paul because he is clever, or even brilliantly clever; I am to bow before St. Paul because he has divine authority; and in any case it remains St. Paul's responsibility to see that he produces that impression, whether anybody bows before his authority or not. St. Paul must not appeal to his cleverness, for in that case he is a fool; he must not enter into a purely aesthetic or philosophical discussion of the content of the doctrine, for in that case he is side-tracked. No, he must appeal to his divine authority and, while willing to lay down his life and everything, by that very means *prevent* any aesthetic impertinence and any direct philosophic approach to the form and content of the doctrine. St. Paul has not to recommend himself and his doctrine with the help of beautiful similes; on the contrary, he should say to the individual: ' Whether the comparison is beautiful or whether it is worn and threadbare is all one, you must realize that what I say was entrusted to me by a revelation, so that it is God Himself or the Lord Jesus Christ who speaks, and you must not presumptuously set about criticizing the form. I cannot and dare not compel you to obey, but through your relation to God in your conscience I make you eternally responsible to God, eternally responsible for your relation to this doctrine, by having proclaimed it as revealed to me, and consequently proclaimed it with divine authority.'

Authority is the decisive quality. Or is there perhaps no difference, even within the relativity of human existence, and even though it disappears in immanence, between the king's command and the word of a poet or a thinker? And what is that difference if not that the king's command has authority and prohibits all aesthetic and critical impertinence as to the form and the content? But neither the poet nor the thinker has authority, even within his own sphere of relativity; their statements are judged on purely aesthetic and philosophic grounds according to the value of the form and the content. The cause of the fundamental confusion in Christianity is surely that as a result of scepticism people are uncertain whether there is a God, and furthermore, that rebelling against all authorities they forget the meaning and dialectic of authority. A king is present physically and one can physically assure oneself of the fact, and should it become necessary he can give one decided physical proof that he is there. But God is not present in that sense. Scepticism has used this fact in order to put God on the same level as all those who have no authority, on the same level as genius, poets and the thinkers, whose sayings are judged from a purely aesthetic or philos-

ophic point of view; and then, if the thing is
well said, the man is a genius—and if it is
unusually well said, then God said it!

In that way God is spirited away. What is
he to do? If God stops a man on the road,
and calls him with a revelation and sends him
armed with divine authority among men, they
say to him: from whom dost thou come? He
answers: from God. But now God cannot
help his messenger physically like a king, who
gives him soldiers or policemen, or his ring or
his signature, which is known to all; in short,
God cannot help men by providing them with
physical certainty that an Apostle is an Apostle
—which would, moreover, be nonsense. Even
miracles, if the Apostle has that gift, give no
physical certainty; for the miracle is the object
of faith. Moreover, it is nonsense to require
physical certainty that an Apostle is an Apostle
(the paradoxical qualification of a spiritual
relationship), just as it is nonsense to require a
physical certainty that God exists, since God is
spirit. The Apostle, then, says he comes from
God. The others answer: Very well, then, let
us see whether the content of your teaching is
divine, in which case we will accept it, along
with the fact that it was revealed to you. In
that way both God and the Apostle are fooled.
The divine authority of the one called should
in fact be the sure protection which safeguards
the teaching, and preserves it at the majestic

distance of the divine from impertinent curiosity,
instead of which the doctrine has to submit to
being criticized and sniffed at—in order that
people may discover whether it was a revelation
or not; and probably in the meanwhile God
and the Apostle have to wait at the gate, or in
the porter's lodge, till the learned upstairs have
settled the matter. The man who is called
ought, according to divine ordinance, to use his
divine authority in order to be rid of all the
impertinent people who will not obey, but want
to reason; and instead of that men have,
at a single go, transformed the Apostle into an
examinee who appears on the market with a
new teaching.

What, then, is authority? Is it the profundity, the excellence, the cleverness of the
doctrine? Not at all! If authority simply
expressed in a higher potency, or reduplicated,
the fact that the doctrine is profound, then
there is no such thing as authority; for in that
case if the learner were to assimilate this
doctrine completely and entirely through the
understanding, then there would cease to be
any difference between the teacher and the
learner. Authority is, on the contrary, something which remains unchanged, which one
cannot acquire even by understanding the
doctrine perfectly. *Authority is a specific quality
which, coming from elsewhere, becomes qualitatively
apparent when the content of the message or of the*

action is posited as indifferent. Let us take an
example, as simple as possible, where the
situation is nevertheless made clear. When a
man with authority says to a man, go! and when
a man who has not the authority says, go! the
expression (go!) and its content are identical;
aesthetically it is, if you like, equally well said,
but the authority makes the difference. If
authority is not ' the other ' (τὸ ἕτερον),[1] if it is
in any sense merely a higher potency within the
identity, then there is no such thing as
authority. If a teacher is enthusiastically
conscious that he has expressed the doctrine
which he is proclaiming at the sacrifice of all
else, this consciousness may well give him
determination, but it does not give him
authority. His life as a proof of the rightness
of the teaching is not ' the other ' (τὸ ἕτερον);
it is a simple reduplication. The fact that he
lives according to the doctrine does not prove
that it is right, but only that because he is
convinced of the righteousness of his teaching
he therefore lives according to it. On the other
hand, whether a police official is a rascal or an

[1] Perhaps it will occur to some readers, as it occurs to me,
to recall in connexion with this examination of ' authority '
the ' Edifying Discourses ' of Magister Kierkegaard, where
he stresses the fact so clearly, by repeating word for word
on each occasion, that ' they are not sermons, because the
author is without authority to preach '. Authority is a
specific quality either of an Apostolic calling or of ordination.
To preach simply means to use authority; and that is exactly
what is completely and utterly forgotten in these times.

upright man—as soon as he is on duty he has
authority.

In order to throw more light on the concept
authority, so important for the sphere of the
paradox-religious, I will elaborate the dialectic
of authority.

*Authority is inconceivable within the sphere of
immanence, or else it can only be thought of as
something transitory.* In so far as one may speak
of authority in political, social, and disciplinary
connexions, or of using authority, authority is
only a transitory factor, a passing thing which
either vanishes later in time, or vanishes in so
far as time and earthly life are transitory factors
which disappear with all their differentiations.
The only difference which can be *conceived* as
the basis for the relations between man and man
qua man is the difference within the identity of
immanence, that is to say essential equality.
The individual man cannot be *conceived* as
differing from all other men by a specific quality
(otherwise all thought would cease, as in fact it
quite consistently does in the sphere of paradox-
religion and of faith). All the human differences
among men *qua* men vanish before thought as
factors within the whole and within the quality
of identity. For the moment it is my duty to
respect and obey the difference, but religiously
I may feel myself edified by the certainty that
the differences disappear in eternity, those that
single me out no less than those which weigh me

down. As a subject it is my duty to honour
and obey the king with undivided heart, but
religiously I may feel strengthened by the
thought that, essentially, I am a citizen of
heaven and that should I ever meet the king
after death I shall no longer be bound to him
by the ties of obedience of a subject.

Such is the position as between man and man
qua man. But between God and man there is an
eternal, essential, qualitative difference which
cannot, at the risk of presumption, be allowed
to disappear in the blasphemous thought that,
though certainly different in the transitory
moment of time, so that man ought to obey and
to pray God in this life, nevertheless the difference will, in eternity, vanish in an essential
identity, so that in eternity God and man, like
king and servant, become equals.

Between God and man, then, there is and
remains an eternal, essential, qualitative difference. *The paradox-religious relationship* (which,
quite rightly, cannot be thought, but only
believed) *appears when God appoints a particular
man to divine authority,* in relation, be it carefully
noted, to that which God has entrusted to him.
The man thus called is no longer related as man
to man *qua* man; his relationship to other men
is not that of a qualitative difference (such as
genius, exceptional gifts, position, &c.), he is
related paradoxically by having a specific
quality which no immanence can resolve in the

equality of eternity; for it is essentially paradoxical and *after* thought (not before, anterior
to thought), contrary to thought. If a man thus
called has a doctrine to bring forth according
to a divine command, and another man, let us
suppose, of himself and by himself discovered
the same thing: then in all eternity the two
things would not become equal; for the first
man is different from every other man by
virtue of his paradoxically specific quality
(divine authority), and different from the
immanently essential equality which is at the
basis of all other human differences. The
qualification ' an Apostle ' belongs in the transcendental sphere, the sphere of paradox-
religion which, quite consistently, also has a
qualitatively different expression for the relation of other men to an Apostle: namely, they
are related to him in faith, whereas thought is
and breathes and has its being in immanence.
But faith is not a transitory qualification, any
more than the Apostle's paradoxical qualification was transitory. Between man and man *qua*
man, then, no *established* or continuous authority
was *conceivable;* it was something transitory.
But for the sake of the essential consideration of
authority, however, we may dwell for a moment
upon a few examples of so-called, and in
temporal conditions true, forms of authority. A
king, it is assumed, has authority. Nevertheless,
there is something disturbing in the idea of a

king who is witty or an artist. The explanation
of this is, surely, that one naturally lays the
stress on his royal authority and so by comparison looks upon the more general human
marks of distinction as something transitory, as
something fortuitous, inessential and disturbing. A government department is regarded as
having authority within its orbit. And yet it
would be disturbing if its ordinances were
really clever, witty, and profound. Here again
the explanation is that, quite rightly, all the
accent falls qualitatively on the authority. To
ask whether a king is a genius—with the
intention, if such were the case, of obeying him,
is in reality *lèse-majesté;* for the question conceals a doubt as to whether one intends to
submit to authority. To be prepared to
obey a government department if it can
be clever is really to make a fool of it. To
honour one's father because he is intelligent is
impiety.

However, as has already been said, between
man and man *qua* man authority, when it exists,
is something transitory, and eternity does away
with all forms of worldly authority. But now,
with regard to the transcendental sphere, let
us take an example, as simple as possible and
for that very reason as striking as can be. When
Christ says, ' There is an eternal life '; and
when a theological student says, ' There is an
eternal life:' both say the same thing, and

there is no more deduction, development, profundity, or thoughtfulness in the first expression
than in the second; both statements are, judged
aesthetically, equally good. And yet there is
an eternal qualitative difference between them!
Christ, as God-Man, is in possession of the
specific quality of authority which eternity can
never mediate, just as in all eternity Christ can
never be put on the same level as essential
human equality. Christ taught, therefore, with
authority. To ask whether Christ is profound
is blasphemy, and is an attempt (whether
conscious or not) to destroy Him surreptitiously;
for the question conceals a doubt concerning
His authority, and this attempt to weigh Him
up is impertinent in its directness, behaving as
though He were being examined, instead of
which it is to Him that all power is given in
heaven and upon earth.

Yet, nowadays, it is seldom, very seldom, that
one hears or reads a religious discourse which is
framed correctly. The better among them often
dabble a little in what one might call un-
conscious or well-meant rebellion, by defending
and upholding Christianity with all their
strength—with the wrong categories. Let me
take an example, the first that comes to hand. I
prefer to choose a German because then I know
that no one, not even the most stupid, not even
the most wrong-headed, could imagine that I
am writing about a matter which in my belief is

infinitely important—in order to point to some
clergyman or other. Bishop Sailer,[1] in a homily
for the Fifth Sunday in Lent, preaches on the
text John viii. 47-51. He chooses these two
verses: ' He that is of God heareth God's word,'
and 'If a man keep my sayings, he shall never
die,' and continues: ' in these words of the
Lord three great mysteries are solved, mysteries
over which men have racked their brains from
the beginning of time '. There we have it.
The word ' mystery ', and particularly the
' three great mysteries ', and then in the next
phase, ' over which men have racked their
brains ', immediately leads one's thoughts on to
the profound in an intellectual sense; ponder-
ing, searching, speculation. Yet how can a
simple apodictic statement be profound, an
apodictic statement which is only what it is
because so and so has said it; a statement which
is not to be understood or fathomed, but simply
believed? How can any man imagine that a
mystery is solved, in a learned speculative way,
by a direct statement, by an assertion? The
question is, after all: Is there an eternal life?
The answer: There is an eternal life. What, in
heaven's name, is profound about that? If
Christ had not said it, and if Christ was not
who He said He was, then if the statement itself
is profound, it must be possible to discover its

[1] J. M. Sailer 1751-1832, Bishop of Regensberg, tutor of
Ludwig I of Bavaria.

profundity. Let us take the example of Herr
Petersen, the theological student, who also says,
' There is an eternal life.' Would it ever strike
any one to tax him with profundity on account
of a direct statement? The decisive thing is not
the statement, but the fact that it was Christ
who said it; but the confusing thing is that, as
though in order to tempt people to believe, they
talk about profundity. In order to speak
correctly a Christian priest would have to say,
quite simply: We have Christ's word for it that
there is an eternal life; and that settles the
matter. There is no question here of racking
one's brains or philosophizing, but simply that
Christ said it, not as a profound thinker but
with divine authority. Let us go further, let us
suppose that a man believes in eternal life on
Christ's word. In that case he believes without
any fuss about being profound and searching
and philosophical and ' racking his brains '. On
the other hand, take the case of a man who
racks his brains and ruminates profoundly on
the question of immortality: would he not be
justified in denying that this direct statement is
a profound answer to the question? What
Plato says on immortality really is profound,
reached after deep study; but then poor Plato
has no authority whatsoever.

In the meanwhile, the thing is this. Doubt
and superstition, which make of faith a vain
thing, have among other things also made men

shy of obedience, of bowing before authority.
This rebelliousness worms its way even into the
thought of better people, perhaps unbeknown
to them, and so begins all the extravagance,
which at bottom is only treachery, about the
profundity and the beauty which one can but
faintly perceive. And so if one had to describe
the Christian-religious discourse as it is now
heard with a single definite predicate, one
would have to say it was *affected*. Normally in
referring to a priest's affectation, one means the
way he dresses, or gets himself up, or that he
talks in a sugary voice, or that he rolls his Rs
like a foreigner, wrinkles his brow, or uses
violent gestures and ridiculous poses. All this,
however, is of less importance, though it is
desirable that he should not do so. But the
pernicious thing is when the whole train of his
thought is affected, when the price of its
orthodoxy is an emphasis in an entirely wrong
place, when he calls for faith in Christ, when he
preaches faith in Him on grounds which simply
cannot be the object of faith. If a son were to
say, ' I obey my father, not because he is my
father but because he is a genius, or because his
orders are always profoundly intelligent,' then
that filial obedience is affected. The son
accentuates something entirely wrong, he
emphasizes the intellectual aspect, the profundity in a *command*, whereas a command is,
of course, indifferent to that qualification. The

son wishes to obey by virtue of the father's
intellectual profundity; and to *obey* by virtue
thereof is just what is not possible, for his
critical attitude as to whether the command is
profound undermines the obedience. And so,
too, it is affectation to speak of adopting
Christianity and believing Christ because of the
great profundity of the doctrine. By putting
the accent in entirely the wrong place one only
makes a show of orthodoxy. The whole of
modern philosophy[1] is therefore affected,
because it has done away with *obedience* on the
one hand, and *authority* on the other, and then,
in spite of everything, claims to be orthodox. A
priest who is quite correct in his discourse
would, when quoting the words of Christ, have
to speak in this way: ' These words were spoken
by Him to whom, according to His own statement, is given all power in heaven and on
earth. You who hear me must consider within
yourselves whether you will bow before his
authority or not, accept and believe the words
or not. But if you do not wish to do so, then for
heaven's sake do not go and accept the words
because they are clever or profound or wonder-
fully beautiful, for that is a mockery of God.'
For, once the command of authority, of the
specific paradox-authority, is posited, then all
relationships are qualitatively changed, then
the kind of acceptance which was previously

---

[1] Contemporary—i.e. Hegel.—Tr.

allowable and desirable becomes a crime and presumptious.

But now how can an Apostle prove that he has authority? If he could prove it *physically*, then he would not be an Apostle. He has no other proof than his own statement. That has to be so; for otherwise the believer's relationship to him would be direct instead of being paradoxical. In the transitory conditions of authority between man and man *qua* man, authority will normally be physically recognizable by power. An Apostle has no other proof than his own statement, and at the most his willingness to suffer anything for the sake of that statement. His words in this respect will be short: ' I am called by God; do with me what you will, scourge me, persecute me, but my last words are my first: I am called by God, and I make you eternally responsible for what you do against me.' Let us suppose that an Apostle were really to have power in the worldly sense, had great influence and powerful connexions, the forces with which one is victorious over men's opinions and judgements —then if he used them he would *eo ipso* have lost his cause. By using power he would have defined his efforts as essentially identical with those of other men, and yet an Apostle is only what he is through his paradoxical heterogeneity, through having divine authority, which he can possess absolutely and unchanged even if he is looked upon by men, as St. Paul says, as less than the filth they walk upon.

(3) *Genius has only an immanent teleology; the Apostle is absolutely, paradoxically, teleologically placed.*

If a man can be said to be situated absolutely teleologically, then he is an Apostle. The doctrine communicated to him is not a task which he is given to ponder over, it is not given him for his own sake, he is, on the contrary, on a mission and has to proclaim the doctrine and use authority. Just as a man, sent into the town with a letter, has nothing to do with its contents, but has only to deliver it; just as a minister who is sent to a foreign court is not responsible for the content of the message, but has only to convey it correctly; so, too, an Apostle has really only to be faithful in his service, and to carry out his task. Therein lies the essence of an Apostle's life of self-sacrifice, even if he were never persecuted, in the fact that he is ' poor, yet making many rich ', that he never dares take the time or the quiet or carefreeness in order to grow rich. Intellectually speaking he is like a tireless housewife who herself hardly has time to eat, so busy is she preparing food for others. And even though at first he might have hoped for a long life, his life to the very end will remain unchanged, for there will always be new people to whom to proclaim the doctrine. Although a revelation is a paradoxical factor which surpasses man's understanding, one can nevertheless understand this much, which has, moreover, proved to be the case everywhere: that a man is called by a revelation to go out in the world, to proclaim the Word, to act and to suffer, to a life of uninterrupted activity as the Lord's messenger. But that a man should be called by a revelation to sit back and enjoy his possessions undisturbed, in active literary *far niente*, momentarily clever, and afterwards as publisher and editor of the uncertainties of his cleverness: that is something approaching blasphemy.[1]

It is otherwise with genius; it has only an immanent teleology, it develops itself, and while developing itself this self-development projects itself as its work. It thus receives importance, perhaps even great importance, but it is not teleologically situated in regard to the world and to others. Genius lives in itself; and, humorously, might live withdrawn and self-satisfied, without for that reason taking its gifts in vain, so long as it develops itself earnestly and industriously, following its own genius, regardless of whether others profit by it or not. Genius is therefore in no sense inactive, and works within itself perhaps harder than a dozen business men put together, but none of its achievements have any exterior *telos*. That is at once the humanity and the pride of

[1] A reference to Mag. Adler. See Introduction, p. 11.

genius: the humanity lies in the fact that it does not define itself teleologically in relation to any other man, as though there were any one who needed it; its pride lies in the fact that it immanently relates itself to itself. It is modest of the nightingale not to require any one to listen to it; but it is also proud of the nightingale not to care whether any one listens to it or not. The dialectic of genius will give particular offence in our times, where the masses, the many, the public, and other such abstractions contrive to turn everything topsy-turvy. The honoured public, the domineering masses, wish genius to express that it exists for their sake; they only see one side of the dialectic of genius, take offence at its pride and do not perceive that the same thing is also modesty and humility. The honoured public and the domineering masses would therefore also take the existence of an Apostle in vain. For it is certainly true that he exists absolutely for the sake of others, is sent out for the sake of others; but it is not the masses and not mankind and not the public, not even the highly educated public, which is his lord and master—but God; and the Apostle is one who has divine authority to command both the masses and the public.

The humorous self-sufficiency of genius is the unity of a modest resignation in the world and a proud elevation above the world: of being an unnecessary superfluity and a precious ornament. If the genius is an artist, then he accomplishes his work of art, but neither he nor his work of art has a *telos* outside him. Or he is an author, who abolishes every teleological relation to his environment and humorously defines himself as a poet. Lyrical art has certainly no *telos* outside it: and whether a man writes a short lyric or folios, it makes no difference to the quality of the nature of his work. The lyrical author is only concerned with his production, enjoys the pleasure of producing, often perhaps only after pain and effort; but he has nothing to do with others, he does not write *in order that:* in order to enlighten men or in order to help them along the right road, in order to bring about something; in short, he does not write *in order that.* The same is true of every genius. No genius has an *in order that;* the Apostle has, absolutely and paradoxically, an *in order that.*